WIN, PLACE AND SHOW

WIN, PLACE AND SHOW

An Introduction to the Thrill of Thoroughbred Racing

Betsy Berns

WIN, PLACE AND SHOW
Copyright © 2001

Published by
Daily Racing Form Press
100 Broadway, 7th Floor
New York, NY 10005-1902

ISBN: 0-9700147-1-6

Cover designed by Chris Donofry
Photos courtesy of Michael J. Martin
Illustrations by Remi Bellocq
Copyedited by Robin Foster
Interior design by Neuwirth and Associates

Printed in the Unites States of America

Acknowledgment

Mandy Minger, Dean Keppler, Peggy Hendershot, and Tim O'Leary, thank you for your enthusiasm, energy, and good humor during this project. I'll miss our weekly conference calls.

I'd also like to thank the following people for their help and support in researching and writing this book: the unforgettable duo (Peter Rotondo and his father, Peter), Laura Hubler, Karl Schmitt, Jennifer Karpf (NSMN), Ashlee Keogh, Doug Reed, John Totaro, Paula Hunt, Lesley Visser, Patricia Barnstable Brown, Brad Free, Jay Privman, Barry Schwartz, Bob Baffert, Jenine Sahadi, Ron Korn, Bill Theodore, Hilary Pridham, Warren Ashenmil, Jamie Haydon, Bryan Pettigrew, Tom Durkin, Dr. Ted Hill, Jerry Bailey, Mike Lakow, Sunny Taylor, Howie Tesher, Donald Morehouse Sr., Monica, Lorna, Brittany, Olga and the students at the University of Arizona. I especially would like to thank the Berns and Korn families, and of course my wonderful husband, Doug, and my two girls, for providing endless inspiration.

Table of Contents

SECOND FURLONG
Exploring Various Racetracks and Race Classifications

THIRD FURLONG
The People Behind the Scenes

FOURTH FURLONG
Daily Racing Form: The Horseplayer's Bible

FIFTH FURLONG
The Thoroughbred Athlete's Key Personnel

Foreword

By Rick Pitino

To take a line from one of my own books, "Hard work and togetherness help us to soar to the next level." In the horse-racing business, nothing could be truer. Until I became actively involved in Thoroughbred ownership, I never realized the camaraderie and teamwork involved with getting these special athletes from the barn to racetrack. Having been blessed with some tremendously talented runners and some of the best "coaches" in the business, like Nick Zito, Shug McGaughey, John Parisella and Cam Gambolati, I've been fortunate enough to see firsthand how a top-notch Thoroughbred-racing program operates. Everybody plays a role in getting these exceptional animals ready for race day. From the hot walker and groom to the trainer and owner, everyone does their share. There's not one position that's more important than the other is. They are all equal and everyone must work together to succeed.

Unfortunately, the casual racing fan rarely has the opportunity to see all the individuals and other elements that make up this wonderful game. Most of the time they only see the finished product. I believe Thoroughbred racing is one of the greatest games in the world and it only takes a little knowledge and exposure to hook a fan for life. It worked for me! As a New York City native, the only horses I ever came in contact with while growing up were the mounted police and the scenic horse-and-carriage rides in Central Park! Now that I'm a full-blown Kentucky resident and Thoroughbred owner, I'm around horses and horse people all the time. I truly love every minute of it.

The horse-racing industry was screaming for a book that takes you behind the scenes and presents this fantastic game in an easy-to-read format that everyone can enjoy. In *Win, Place and Show,* author Betsy Berns has done just that in her wonderfully presented introduction to the thrill of Thoroughbred racing. Not only do you get to learn the rich tradition and history of the game, but also, Berns does a great job of presenting helpful information that both the novice and seasoned racing fan can utilize. The book is full of material on the breeding and sale of horses, memorable racing moments, and jockey, trainer, and owner interviews. Most importantly, you can find out how to read the *Daily Racing Form*, place some bets, and fatten your wallet! I hope to see you at the races.

Welcome to the Thrill of Thoroughbred Racing

HORSE RACING FANS are a diverse group. Some have been coming to the track since they were very young while others are casual fans and only watch the Kentucky Derby the first Saturday in May. This book is designed for racing fans of all levels. From the novice fan to the seasoned expert, the book has something for everyone. If you've never been to the track, this book will help you learn enough of the basics to make you feel comfortable about watching and betting on your first race. And if you're a seasoned veteran, you can read this book for the interviews, fun facts, and insights from the people who know horses and racing best.

The book is divided into furlongs (like a typical horse race). For easy reference and an enjoyable read, the book is littered with fun facts, helpful hints, and "betting window" asides to help you extract important information at a glance. These boxes give you tips, predictions, and interesting information that will help you decipher what's going on at the racetrack. This will not only make you more knowledgeable about the game, but also make your racetrack experience more memorable. There are also many beautiful photos and illustrations that help bring to life the information that fills these chapters.

Feel free to follow along in the book at your own pace. The first furlong (chapter 1-5) will give you a basic education in horse racing.

The first few chapters explain the physical makeup of a horse and take you through the history of the sport. You will then learn about the breeding process and a horse's training schedule.

The second furlong explores the racetracks and explains race classifications. The third furlong includes interviews with people behind the scenes at the track, including the groom, track veterinarian, and track announcer. The fourth furlong covers some of the important information needed for effectively reading past-performance data and placing wagers at the track.

The fifth furlong takes you into the lives of the jockey, trainer, and owner, with first-person accounts of their day-to-day schedules. By the sixth furlong you'll be ready to hear about how to maximize your day at the races and how to throw a Kentucky Derby bash.

In the seventh furlong, a racing secretary gives you insights into his job.

Now you're ready for the homestretch, where you'll learn about the Triple Crown races (the Kentucky Derby, Preakness, and Belmont) as well as one of the greatest days in racing—the Breeders' Cup. To wrap it all up, you'll read about some of racing's legendary champions and have a strong taste of what this great sport is all about. I guarantee you're in for an exciting ride. Enjoy!

The Wonderful World of Thoroughbred Horse Racing

1

Discovering
Thoroughbred Racing

THE TOTAL ATHLETE

THOROUGHBRED-RACING FANS fall in love with this ancient sport for reasons as numerous and different as the days of the racing season. For many devotees, the lure is the unique pageantry of the track, which bombards and excites the senses. Racing offers a dazzling array of sensory treats—the bright patterns of racing colors, the smell of fresh-cut grass in the paddock, the familiar bugle cry calling the horses to the post, the roar of the crowd, punctuated by frantic individual pleas for victory, the warmth of the sun beating down on the grandstand on a spring afternoon, the soothing wetness of a tall glass of iced tea or a mint julep in the clubhouse, the heart-racing, ground-shaking pounding of hooves thundering down the homestretch, and the glint of pride in the eye of a champion Thoroughbred in the winner's circle.

Others become attached to the sport due to its gaming element. Thoroughbred racing is unique among major American sports in the extent to which wagering is an integral part of the sport and is enjoyed legally. Betting on a horse ties together the fortunes of the fan, the horse, and the jockey for the duration of the race, bringing to the fan a feeling of participation and a level of excitement rare among spectator sports. The tracks offer betting options for all tastes—some conservative and simple, others remote in probability but offering the lure of a big payoff.

Still other people simply love horses and enjoy watching these regal equine athletes do what they do best—run like the wind with a grace unequaled. Many fans were first attracted to racing by the performance of a specific horse or some other early memorable racing moment, such as those provided by the legendary Triple Crown winner Secretariat. This champion's champion was the only horse ever to have graced the cover of *Sports Illustrated*. His unforgettable combination of heart, strength, and sheer athletic ability was unmatched in his day. Secretariat's talent on the racetrack was best illustrated by his statement-making 31-length victory in the 1973 Belmont Stakes, and his earlier record-setting triumph in the 99th running of the Kentucky Derby, in which he ran 1 1/4 miles in 1:59 2/5, a mark that still stands. Previous generations of Thoroughbred-racing enthusiasts may have cheered Man o' War's impressive 20 victories from 21 starts or Citation's unprecedented 3-year-old season. If you have been fortunate enough to be part of a momentous racing event such as any of these, there's an excellent chance that racing has been in your blood ever since.

MY FIRST EXPERIENCE

OF COURSE, THERE ARE ALSO the fans that have a great experience at the track early on and get hooked immediately. I fall into this category and had an exciting (and not that unusual) rookie fan experience.

Many first-timers go to the track and impulsively bet on horses for whimsical reasons: a favorite number or combination, the horse's appearance, the colors of the jockey's silks, or a name that holds some unique personal significance. More often than you might think, these types of horses end up winning!

I had one of these experiences. While visiting Southern California, I spent a sunny afternoon at the beautiful Del Mar racetrack south of San Diego. As I entered the stands, the day's second race was about to start. Anxious to enter the ranks of experienced bettors, I trotted up to a ticket window, rapidly scanned the list of horses running, and immediately placed a bet on one of the entrants in the field. I made my highly unscientific choice because the horse's name reminded me of an ancient saying that I always liked: "All glory is fleeting." (The corollary to that saying, by the way, is that "mediocrity is forever.") After placing my bet I strolled over to the rail to watch the race. When I glanced up at the tote board I learned that I had just bet on a 20-1 longshot. I felt foolish for making such an uninformed choice, and vowed not to tell anyone.

The race began and, much to my surprise, my 20-1 shot got off to a good start and was holding his own among ostensibly better and faster competitors. My spirits began to pick up as my horse refused to fade and was among the leaders going into the homestretch. I will never forget the rush that I felt as my longshot muscled his way to the head of the pack and pulled out the unexpected win. Not only did I collect a bundle of money, but I also felt like the craftiest handicapper in the world. I didn't win again the rest of the day, but I was still hooked. It wasn't just the money, but the whole racing experience that was a delight.

I have to admit that I was a bit intimidated by the track at first. Sure, there were plenty of other newcomers in attendance, but there were also lots of hard-core fans with their heads buried in the *Daily Racing Form*. Many of these fans acted like the track was their second home. My knowledge of handicapping consisted of the terms win, place, and show.

That's when it occurred to me that to further enjoy my track experience, I would like to learn a lot more about the sport and the industry behind it. I wanted to be able to comfortably converse with other fans, and to learn why Thoroughbred horse racing is called the Sport of Kings.

I spoke with other novice fans, who agreed that they also would like to learn more, which eventually led to my decision to write this book. The key to making your racetrack experience more enjoyable, and hopefully more profitable, is to familiarize yourself with *all* the components involved in the sport. As with any new hobby or game, you begin by learning the basics and working your way forward. I invite you to hold on to your seat (or should I say saddle!) and come along for the ride.

2

The Physical Makeup of the Racehorse:
Understanding Conformation

T IS OFTEN SAID IN SPORTS that great athletes aren't just born that way. Thoroughbreds, however, may be a notable exception to this conventional wisdom. Thoroughbreds are bred to be athletes. They are the result of the best available stallions matched to the most suitable mares. The Thoroughbred racehorse is designed for speed. If you break down the word *Thoroughbred*, you get *thorough*, which means "complete," and the verb *bred*, which means "to raise or reproduce." The ultimate goal of every Thoroughbred breeder is to create the complete athlete. Hundreds of years of successful breeding have done just that. Thoroughbreds are capable of running top speeds of 30 to 40 miles per hour for substantial distances while carrying jockeys.

There is a downside to this selective breeding. Next time you examine a Thoroughbred during the post parade, look closely at its legs and body. The big, muscular body sits on top of powerful but

Proper conformation and physical soundness determine the Thoroughbred's ability to run effectively on the racetrack.

very fragile legs. Like any great athlete, the Thoroughbred suffers stress fractures, muscle pulls, tendon strains, and many other types of physical ailments. It has been specifically bred to perfect the speed of its very swift legs. Unfortunately, selective breeding has not uniformly produced horses whose legs are stronger and less fragile. The legs are the lifeblood of this animal. Therefore, trainers and grooms are careful to give the Thoroughbred's legs and feet the special attention they require, which usually includes wrapping, massaging, and soaking them before and after a workout or race.

CONFORMATION

THE CONFORMATION OF A Thoroughbred includes its overall appearance and structure. The Thoroughbred's body shape and structure affect both speed and stamina. While conformation can be somewhat subjective, there are still some traditional characteristics that experts use to make decisions regarding a Thoroughbred's probable physical soundness. Some base their assessment of soundness on how straight a horse's angles and lines are to his body. They will look for good balance, muscle tone, and bone structure. Experts will also pay attention to how graceful a horse looks when it walks, and whether its legs and feet are straight. While the legs are an extremely important part of its structure, the Thoroughbred also requires a strong back, shoulders, and hindquarters to run correctly and efficiently. The horse's hindquarters are usually the best indicator of its speed potential. A horse with wide hindquarters usually has more pure speed than horses with narrow ones.

Every horse has some physical imperfections. The handicapper, breeder, owner, and trainer must pick and choose which factors they believe to be the most influential in predicting a horse's running potential. Some professionals will look seriously at a horse's knees, while others might consider a horse's neck or shoulders as important variables.

The Anatomy of Racing

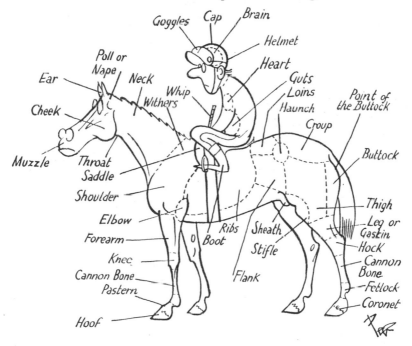

COLOR

THE COLOR OF THE THOROUGHBRED is not a factor in determining its racing ability. Racing fans, however, may have their own preferences in that area, and may even base their betting selections on color alone. For example, some casual fans enjoy betting on gray horses. Thoroughbred owners, breeders, and trainers have their favorite colors, too, but are more concerned about a horse's pedigree and racing potential.

Fun Fact

The Thoroughbred comes in a variety of colors. A *bay* horse is brown with a black mane and tail. A *chestnut* is reddish in color. A *gray* or roan-colored horse has white hairs that are intermixed with a darker color. A *dark bay* or *brown* appears almost black in color. The truly *black* horse is rare and the *white* horse is even more rare.

Fun Fact

It's an old wives' tale that one white foot on a horse is considered good luck, and an indication that it will be a fast runner.

HEIGHT, STRUCTURE, AND ATTITUDE

THROUGH SELECTIVE BREEDING, the Thoroughbred has inherited a fiercely competitive nature. This competitiveness, combined with determination and (ideally) a winning attitude, shapes the complete racehorse. Centuries ago, wild horses had to run from their predators. Even through years of domestication, horses have never lost that instinct. From the day a horse is born, his first instinct is to run. This explains why you'll see a foal attempt to stand up just minutes after birth. In addition, the foal must get to its feet and nurse in order to receive the colostrum—found in its mother's milk—that is essential to develop its immune system. Farms keep colostrum "banks" in case a mare cannot nurse her foal.

HELPFUL HINT

A hand is four inches. A horse's height is measured from the ground to the highest point of the withers (the ridge between the shoulder bones of the horse), which is located at the top of the shoulders, just in front of the saddle.

Most Thoroughbreds are fairly similar in height and weight. In general, adult Thoroughbreds measure 15.3 to 16.3 hands and weigh between 900 and 1,200 pounds. They possess long, lean muscles, which are interspersed with short, taut muscles for maximum length and power of stride. They have huge lungs to help with their stamina and they enjoy a very high metabolism.

A Thoroughbred that is too short or too tall has both advantages and disadvantages on the racetrack. A bigger, taller horse may not break from the gate as quickly as a smaller one, and may need to be placed in longer-distance races to run to its full potential. A tall, bulky horse may also have great difficulty maneuvering around racetracks that have sharp turns. The taller horse will often perform better on a racing oval that has wide, sweeping turns and a long straightaway. These types of tracks will give the taller horse a better opportunity to reach full stride during the stretch run.

Fun Fact

Some horses, like some people, don't fit the usual measurements. Forego, a three-time Horse of the Year, measured 17 hands tall, while legendary horses War Admiral and Seabiscuit measured less than 15.3 hands.

A shorter, smaller horse is usually quicker from the gate and sometimes has a distinct advantage in sprint races. It may perform better on racetracks that have tighter turns. A shorter horse can get itself in full stride quickly and can avoid being blocked or impeded during the early stages of a race. This advantage can ultimately determine the difference between performing well or poorly.

HEART OF GOLD

THE MOST DISTINGUISHING CHARACTERISTIC of a horse is not physically apparent and might seem intangible. But if you're in the business and around horses all the time, you'll see it in all the "great ones." It's referred to as *heart*. The best athletes of the breed will run as hard as possible and refuse to give up. Like any superior athlete, they hate to lose and will go to extremes to prove victorious.

IMPORTANT BREEDING TERMINOLOGY

UNFORTUNATELY, IT'S NOT ENOUGH just to refer to a horse as a Thoroughbred. As with any sport, there are a few terms that you need to know to help make you sound like a professional. A short list of common Thoroughbred gender-related terms appears below.

HELPFUL HINT

When a mare is sent to breed, she is referred to as a broodmare. She becomes a dam when her first foal is born, and a producer when her first foal competes in its first race.

Blue Hen: A mare that is an exceptional producer of stakes winners.

Broodmare: A filly or mare that no longer races and is used to produce foals.

Broodmare Sire (Damsire): The sire of a broodmare (think maternal grandsire or "grandfather" of a foal).

Colt: A young male horse. Thoroughbreds remain colts through age 4.

Dam: The female parent of a foal (think "mom").

Filly: A young female horse. Thoroughbreds are fillies through age 4.

Foal: A baby horse.

Foundation Mare: A mare that played a key role in establishing her owner as a successful breeder.

Gelding: A castrated male horse. It's rare to see a horse with impressive breeding potential gelded. Sometimes unruly horses will be gelded to make them more consistent and mild-mannered.

Inbred: When the same ancestor appears more than once in a horse's pedigree, particularly in the first four to five generations.

Mare: An adult female horse.

Nick: The combination of two family lines in a pedigree, often resulting in a successful racing offspring.

Outcross: A horse that has no inbreeding, particularly in the first four or five generations.

Sire: The male parent of a foal (think "dad").

Stallion: An adult male horse used for breeding.

Suckling: A foal that is still nursing, therefore the name.

Weanling: A foal that has been separated from its dam, which usually occurs around six months after birth.

Yearling: A horse between his first and second birthdays.

HELPFUL HINT

When a horse is sent to stud, he becomes a stallion. When one of the stallion's offspring (called *get* or *progeny*) wins a race, he's called a sire.

3

An Introduction to
the History of
Thoroughbred Racing

THE UNIQUE BOND BETWEEN MAN AND HORSE

MAN HAS HELD THE RACEHORSE in awe throughout history. The horse's sheer speed, strength and beauty have long fascinated societies and cultures across the world. In prehistoric times, man hunted horses for food. In the horses original home, North America, overhunting by man eventually led to his extinction on its native continent. Later, it was discovered that horses were better utilized as a means of convenient transportation (particularly in times of war). After the fall of the Roman

Empire, Bedouin tribes began training and breeding horses for stamina and speed. These two qualities were essential elements of the "total" racehorse. The Arabs were so serious about pedigree that inbreeding between their best stock became standard practice.

On another continent, the English were breeding horses that were strong and durable. These horses were used for carrying significant amounts of weight. It wasn't until the 1600s, when Englishmen found more time for leisure activities, that horse racing grew in popularity. The nobility of England became passionate about the sport and devoted much of their time to breeding horses specifically for racing. Recognizing that they needed a substantial improvement in the quality of their own stock, the English imported 160 horses from Arabia to breed with their mares. Only those horses that had already

The post parade allows the fan to see how his or her race selection looks on the track at close range.

The History of Thoroughbred Racing

proven themselves on the track were allowed to become a permanent part of the English breeding program. The offspring produced by these horses were also required to run well. If they didn't perform up to par, they were no longer used for breeding. The ultimate result of this process was that today, every Thoroughbred racehorse descends from one of three imported stallions: the Darley Arabian, the Godolphin Arabian, or the Byerley Turk.

THE SPORT OF KINGS

HORSE RACING BEGAN LONG BEFORE the first recorded race. There's no record of the first horse race, but historians believe that it occurred about 5,000 years ago somewhere in central Asia. The first recorded horse race occurred somewhere in Greece before 1200 B.C. By the time of the Trojan wars, racing had become a well-established sport. A Greek warrior, Diomedes, won an important chariot race, which would later go down as the first race in the record books. It wasn't until 776 B.C., however, when the Greeks founded the first Olympic games, that chariot racing with mules took center

stage. By 680 B.C., chariot events became a regular part of the games, and started to entice the interest of royalty. The Romans were even more passionate about racing than the Greeks. The sport, which often attracted thousands of spectators, developed into an organized event during the Roman era.

Fun Fact

Legend has it that Emperor Nero was a huge racing fan, but his wife did not approve of his favorite pastime. Instead of apologizing or making excuses for his love of horse racing, Nero killed his wife.

It is believed that the first racetrack on British soil owed its origin to a Roman emperor, Lucius Septimius Severus, who led a campaign in to Britain. Centuries later, England's Henry VIII was a huge racing fan, and can be credited with being one of the founders of modern racing. Henry required that his dukes maintain his highly structured racing stables. His daughter Elizabeth also enjoyed racing. However, it wasn't until the time of Charles II and James I that racing became known as the Sport of Kings. Their enthusiasm for horse racing was unsurpassed. The term would later become part of racing vernacular because so many kings, rulers, and even presidents developed an interest in the sport.

Fun Fact

Roman Emperor Caligula was so passionate about racing that he bestowed the title and honor of Senator on one of his beloved horses.

The stallions Herod, Matchem, and Eclipse were descendents of the three founding sires mentioned earlier, and each had a further impact on future Thoroughbred-racing lines. Of these three horses,

The History of Thoroughbred Racing

Eclipse was one of the most famous and influential. He was undefeated in 18 career starts, and was responsible for the development
of more than 80 percent of all modern Thoroughbreds.

Fun Fact

In 1773, the General Stud Book, Vol. 1, was released. It
served as a crucial and accurate record of pedigrees for
breeding and identification purposes.

RACING ARRIVES IN AMERICA

WHEN THE ENGLISH ARRIVED in America, they brought along their
enthusiasm for racing. During the 18th century, the breeding of
imported horses took on some importance. However, it wasn't
until the 19th century that American breeders began to really
understand the amount of work involved with breeding successful
racing stock.

In 1798, the English shipped the first Epsom Derby winner,
Diomed, to America. Since Diomed was 21, an elderly age for a
horse, the English had little faith in his breeding potential. Fortunately
for the United States, Diomed produced exceptionally well for 10
years and created a substantial amount of noteworthy racehorses.
One of Diomed's offspring included his fabulous great-grandson
Lexington. Lexington was the most influential Thoroughbred of the
19th century. He appears in the pedigrees of almost every stakes-race
winner in the world today.

HELPFUL HINT

The American Jockey Club has published the American
Stud Book since 1896. It now has more than 3 million horses currently registered in its database.

There were many factors that contributed to the popularity of horse racing in America. The introduction of formal betting, the creation of the American Stud Book in 1868, and the formation of the American Jockey Club in 1894, all helped the sport take off. Although racing continued to grow in America, it still had room for further improvement. The English Jockey Club claimed that the General Stud Book produced in Great Britain was far more accurate than the American book, and therefore had more legitimacy. American racing was also coming under fire because of gambling activities. When the gambling scare subsided and racing started again, the American breeder was forced to import foreign horses (which were superior to the English-bred horses). In 1949, when the English Jockey Club realized that the American horses had excelled beyond their own, they repealed their restrictions in the Stud Book on breeding with American horses.

The History of Thoroughbred Racing

On April 23, 1943, Judy Johnson was granted a license to ride in steeplechase races in Maryland, making her one of the earliest female jockeys.

Cigar was just one of America's modern-day racing heroes. He was a two-time Horse of the Year and retired with nearly $10 million in career earnings.

HELPFUL HINT

The American Stud Book documents the identity of every thoroughbred horse that is bred to compete.

Jockey Julie Krone's riding success set a new standard for all female jockeys.

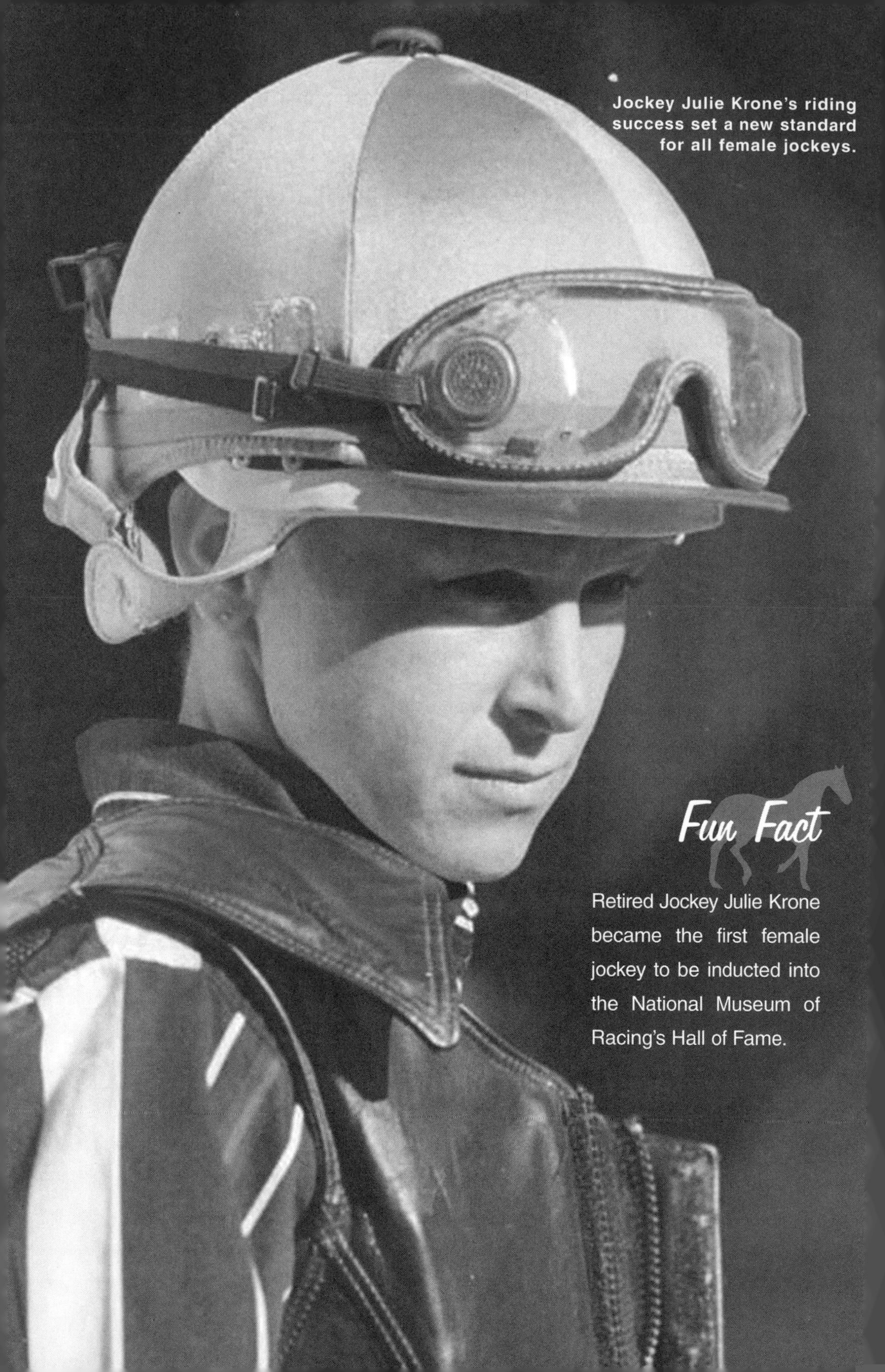

Fun Fact

Retired Jockey Julie Krone became the first female jockey to be inducted into the National Museum of Racing's Hall of Fame.

RACING STARS FROM THE PAST AND PRESENT

As with any form of entertainment, the personalities involved in horse racing add to its attractiveness. Many unique owners, trainers, jockeys, and especially the horses have captured the interests and passions of racing fans. Horses like Man o'War, Citation, Kelso, Secretariat and Cigar have inspired great emotions and fan support. Famous jockeys such as the legendary Bill Shoemaker, Laffit Pincay, and Jerry Bailey, along with trainers D. Wayne Lukas, Bob Baffert,

Hall of Fame jockey Bill Shoemaker.

Man o' War became the first horse to be embalmed and buried in a casket lined with his owner's racing colors.

and Allen Jerkens, have gradually attracted a faithful group of racing fans and enthusiasts over the years. The sport has come a long way since its regal beginning, and Thoroughbred racing has justifiably established itself as one of the most popular spectator sports in the world.

Trainer D. Wayne Lukas.

The popularity of the famous racehorse Secretariat swept across the United States and eventually earned him the honor of having his own U.S. Postal Service stamp.

Horse-racings superstar Secretariat captures the second leg of the Triple Crown — the 1973 Preakness Stakes.

4

The Breeding Shed:
The Making of a Champion

ONGOING FAN SUPPORT

As YOU MAY have already guessed, Thoroughbred horse racing is not like any other sport. For example, if you're a football fan, you might follow a few players during their college playing days. If you're an obsessed fan, you may even observe certain promising players while they're still in high school. You may cheer for them to be selected by your favorite pro teams in the NFL, and continue to follow their careers while they bounce from team to team.

In horse racing, as a true fan, you probably won't start rooting for a specific horse until he is 2 years old. This is the age at which the Thoroughbred is eligible to begin his racing career. He will already have a name and most of his initial training will be completed. You may even discover a promising 2-year-old colt or filly making his debut from one of your favorite trainer's barns. Or, better yet, you might find a juvenile colt or filly that is the offspring of one of your favorite sires or dams. If you are actively involved in the breeding

Thoroughbred auctions draw potential owners from all over the world.

and ownership side of the racing business, you may fall in love with a horse while observing it at a yearling sale. These athletes can grab your attention at any age or stage of their careers. While no two Thoroughbreds act or appear the same, each goes through similar steps of development.

THE BIRTH OF A STAR

THERE ARE TWO kinds of breeding operations: commercial (market) breeders and home breeders. The former sell the offspring of their mares while the latter keep the offspring to race on their behalf, although most commercial breeders also keep a few horses and race them in their own name. Most foals are born during the spring months (March, April, May), which means the mating took place the previous spring. As you might imagine, breeding farms are very busy during these three months. Since so many foals have March, April, or May births, it might seem like a tremendous work overload for these farms. This is not the case at all, however, as each breeding is a carefully planned event.

Every January 1, all Thoroughbreds born during the previous year celebrate their first birthday, regardless of whether they were born in February or on December 31. All racehorses have the same birthday, even though it is possible for a horse to be born any day of the year. It makes no difference whether the horse is three months old, eight months old, or two days old; on January 1 of the following year, he turns one year old. With this in mind, breeders try to have all matings completed by late spring/early summer, to avoid having foals that are much younger than their peers.

Champion Seattle Slew was a yearling-sale bargain.

The Making of a Champion

Once a foal is born, its first instinct is to run. Horses still possess a self-protection instinct from when they used to live in the wild and were prime targets for predators. When a foal was born, predators could smell the birth and would try and attack the newborn. Somehow sensing the danger, the newborn foal would stand up, ready to run as fast as its little wobbly legs could take him. This survival instinct is just another example of how the Thoroughbred became such a swift runner.

HELPFUL HINT

Claiborne Farm, Taylor Made, and Gainesway Farm are just a few of the most prominent breeding operations.

Horses have an 11-month pregnancy.

DOES AGE MATTER?

IN THOROUGHBRED RACING, age does matter. A 2-year-old Thoroughbred with a very late birth date can be at a distinct disadvantage on the racetrack, especially if he is scheduled to race early in the year. Conversely, a racehorse with an early birth date has an advantage both mentally and physically. Each horse matures at a slightly different rate. Some horses are physically and mentally ready for the demands of the racetrack at age 2, while others take many more months or even years to reach full maturity. A lot depends on the horse's pedigree and whether his trainer has had prior success with preparing juvenile horses. (See Chapter 5)

Most horses reach their full potential from the second half of their 3-year-old season through their 5-year-old season; however, many continue to run competitively much longer. Most 2-year-olds race at shorter distances than their elders do. A typical juvenile race early in the year is between four and 5 ½ furlongs. A young colt or filly gradually builds to longer distances as it gains experience and stamina.

A furlong is an eighth of a mile. It's the main unit of measurement for racing in North America and Great Britain.

SEX

MOST THOROUGHBRED RACES are segregated by sex. There is some speculation as to which sex is faster on the track. Many people involved in racing believe that males are faster. While fillies and mares can compete in most types of races, they do have races scheduled exclusively for them. In general, both sexes are fairly equal in ability and competitiveness.

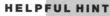

Fun Fact

Most Thoroughbreds are born between midnight and 3:00 a.m.

HELPFUL HINT

All Thoroughbreds inherit their black skin color from their Arabian ancestors.

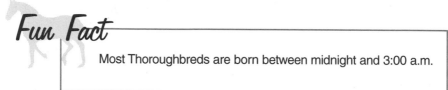

Fun Fact

Around 5:30 a.m. at most breeding farms, there is likely to be music blaring into the stalls. It's important for the horses to get used to hearing loudspeakers, which are very common at future racing venues.

HELPFUL HINT

Thoroughbreds aren't just sold as yearlings. They can be sold at any age or stage of their careers.

WHEN FOALS TURN one year old, they become eligible for yearling sales. Not every yearling can qualify for one of the distinguished sales. The horse must have the proper combination of pedigree and conformation to become one of the chosen few. Buying a yearling for an exorbitant amount of money does not guarantee a winner. Therefore, these sales can sometimes make or break an owner.

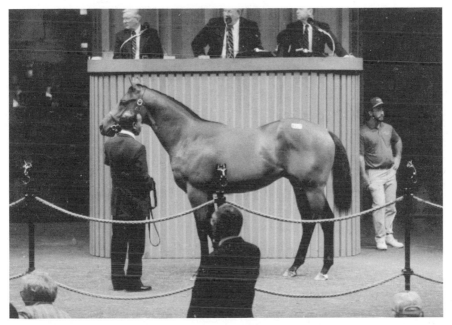

It's not that uncommon for some highly regarded yearlings with premium pedigrees to be sold for well over a million dollars.

Fun Fact

The July sales at Keeneland and Fasig-Tipton in Lexington, Kentucky, and the Fasig-Tipton sale in Saratoga Springs, New York, in August are three of the most prestigious yearling auctions.

Fun Facts

In the year 2000, the total sales at Keeneland's September auction posted a record total of $291,827,100. This topped the previous September-sale record of $233,020,800 set in 1999, and ranked second only to the $317,666,000 spent at Keeneland's 1999 November Breeding Stock Sale. The average, $88,085, and number of horses sold, 3,313, also were records for September. The previous highs were 3,011 horses sold for an average of $77,390, set during the 1999 sale.

∩

Since yearlings have never actually raced before, their value can often be subjective. For example, Seattle Slew, one of the all-time winningest horses, sold for a measly $17,500. This was a true bargain since he earned $1,208,726 in his career.

∩

A horse that has had a successful career on the track can reward his owner with big bucks in the breeding shed. For example, 2000 Kentucky Derby winner Fusaichi Pegasus retired to Ashford Stud for the 2001 breeding season, with a stud fee of $150,000.

Horses will normally not begin training until at least September of their yearling year. They are not mature enough (physically and mentally) until then. The big yearling sales take place in July, August, and September.

AUCTIONS

If you are looking to purchase a horse at an auction, it's important to bring along someone who understands horse conformation and health issues. Many people hire their own experts (veterinarians or trainers) to come to the sales with them to observe the horses. The cost of employing a veterinarian to take a cursory look at a horse varies greatly. Potential bidders may also avail themselves of a repository of the X-rays of all the horses for sale. If you want more extensive probing, which includes more X-rays after the sale, it could be even more costly. A buyer has about 24 hours after the sale to examine and possibly return the horse if he discovers a bone chip or some other major physical problem. Any potential buyer must establish credit with the sale company prior to the auction.

ECONOMIC ISSUES OF OWNING HORSES

Assuming you purchase a horse, you must then decide where to keep him for the next year or so. Some farms are less expensive than others. For example, if you decided to keep the horse in Ocala, Florida, which is less expensive than Kentucky, you might be looking at $14 a day just for housing. If you multiply that by 30 to 31 days, add in the blacksmith bill, and tack on a few other assorted expenses, you are probably averaging about $500 per month. If you decide to keep the horse there for a year, it would cost approximately $6,000. Once the horse goes into training, the price jumps to about $35 per day. If you keep a horse from the time he is taken from his mother until he races as a 2-year-old, you're probably looking at around $15,000.

HELPFUL HINT

Pinhookers are people who buy horses specifically for the purpose of reselling them.

Many people continue to have a relationship with their horses even after they've sold them. This sometimes happens because they've developed a particular fondness for the horse or simply because they want to see if they made a mistake in selling him based on his win/loss racing percentages.

5

The Training Game

AFTER A YEARLING is purchased, he will officially start training for his race debut. Training Thoroughbreds is a process of developing them both mentally and physically, and bringing out their natural abilities. Every horse trains differently, depending on his temperament and experiences during the first year of life. Some horses need extra time to feel comfortable with the new people handling them, while others require extra time to familiarize themselves with the bridle and bit. Still others need more time to master the exercise ring and adjust to jogging and carrying a rider.

The Thoroughbred has to develop many important skills. One of these skills includes mastering a "flying change of lead." When a horse is running, the lead leg reaches out the farthest and bears the most weight. A racehorse usually leads with his right foreleg on a straightaway and changes to the left foreleg on a turn. By doing so, the horse develops all of his muscles, thus allowing him better overall performance; also, changing leads gives the horse a "breather" when one leg gets tired.

Training would not be complete without the horse going through extensive starting-gate exercises. Races can be won or lost simply by how a horse breaks from the starting gate. Therefore, trainers spend a good deal of time developing this specialized skill. At some point in the horse's second year, barring injury or some other setback, it will be ready to go to the track to begin his racing destiny.

A horse must go through extensive starting-gate exercises before he can compete in an actual race (pictured here).

Jenine Sahadi became the first woman trainer to win a Breeders' Cup race and runs a successful West Coast stable. Sahadi gained national attention in 2000 when a horse she trained, The Deputy, won the Grade I Santa Anita Derby and competed in the Kentucky Derby. Sahadi describes what it takes to condition and train a Thoroughbred from the time it arrives at her barn to the end of its racing career.

Jenine Sahadi and one of her top stakes caliber horses, The Deputy.

TRAINING 2-YEAR-OLDS

WHEN A HORSE first arrives at my barn, I give it a simple evaluation to make sure he's sound. You need to continually keep an eye on his maturity level. Some 2-year-olds are more precocious and mentally mature than others, and some require much more time. You need to go very slowly with the young ones. When you first meet the 2-year-olds, you hope that they broke well in their first year. With 2-year-olds, little setbacks always happen. They either have problems with their shins or they have illnesses. The horses have been at a farm and haven't left their familiar grounds until you load them into the big truck. Understandably, this can be a huge culture shock. It's a lot of very slow training. You need to let them become accustomed to their new environment and get them reacquainted with the saddle. You also need to make sure that the exercise rider is really patient in doing everything that he's supposed to do to teach the horse and communicate with him (with your help). It's a lot of jogging, a lot of galloping, and making sure they have a good foundation in them before you start working them. You also need to know when to back off of them if anything comes up. Once they get working, it becomes very apparent if they're interested in doing what they are doing at a young age.

It's just like people. You have a lot of kids who develop quicker. They are sharper and go through the motions in preschool, kindergarten, and right up into grade school. There are other kids that are a little bit slower. Some kids are very brave and others are a little cowardly and shy. You treat your horses just like you would people. They all have different and unique personalities. Some can handle a lot more than others can, and some can sustain a much tougher training regimen. Some are more fragile and light. There are many other things that come into play; the horse's weight, temperament, and how he eats.

UNORTHODOX? YES. BUT **NO ONE** GETS 'EM USED TO THE DIRT LIKE BOB.

TRAINING AND CONDITIONING 3-YEAR-OLDS

I DON'T REALLY do anything differently with 3-year-olds. I just train each horse the way I think he needs to be trained. However, I do think they need a break if they are precocious 2-year-olds and already have four or five races under their belt. As 2-year-olds, it's important to give them a rest before you head into their 3-year-old season. They are athletes and you can't expect them to go full throttle 365 days a year. They will ultimately get tired and burnt out, and will likely back off of their feed. Every horse deserves some time off during the course of a season, regardless of his age.

OLDER HORSES

ONCE THEY GET older and they are fit, they kind of just train themselves. You're more concerned with keeping a horse sound.

FEEDING HORSES

EACH HORSE EATS a little bit differently. Some horses will eat what others don't. When they arrive, regardless of whether they're young or old, it's always fun to try and figure out what they'll eat. I get a lot of ex-European horses, and trying to come up with a scenario that they like food-wise is always interesting. European horses eat completely different foods. The weather and climate are completely different over there. Some will want their food cooked and others don't. Some will eat greens and others like the sweet feed. So, you do a lot of experimenting. Once you find something that they like, as long as they are eating well and cleaning their tub, you don't change their program. I also like to add a little red wine to their food to give it a little flavor. Initially, I started adding wine because I had a crazy horse named Lit de Justice, who was as bad an actor as I have ever been around. Despite his personality, he did win a Breeders' Cup race. I asked my vet if there was anything I could do to take the edge off and he recommended a little red wine (one-quarter to one-half cup). Then I found that a bunch of them liked it so I figured it was a good little treat for them. You can buy it cheap at Price Club for $4.99 a gallon.

DAILY SCHEDULE

WE USUALLY GET to the track every day between 4:30 and 5:00 a.m. There are no holidays (horses have to eat every day, so there's really no time off). You train Christmas, Thanksgiving, and New Year's morning. You have to be willing to accept that you have very little social life, and resign yourself to the fact that you are going to go to bed very early. Every day is generally the same routine with only a few minor differences. In the morning, the first thing you do is check over each horse for soundness. You want to make sure their temperatures are normal and they have eaten all their dinner. Hopefully, you will find few problems that require veterinary attention.

After that, you basically start your morning. For me, I typically work horses every six days, weather permitting. If it starts raining, things change and your schedule gets backed up. You have to be flexible and patient. For example, if you were planning on working a horse and you get up in the morning to find his foot is hot or the horse isn't moving quite right, the work gets delayed. It's a lot of adjustment, and things change quickly. After I work a horse, I walk him the next day. I then usually jog him the following day and gallop him for three or four days before I work him again.

SCHOOL'S IN SESSION

AFTER 10:00 a.m., we do what we call schooling. If today is Wednesday and I have a horse running Friday, I will take him over to the saddling paddock and refamiliarize him with the area. I'll make sure he is comfortable and he is not sweating or getting anxious. You want them to be really comfortable in their environment. Some need two days and some need up to five days of schooling. For the remainder of the day, we usually talk to owners and do some PR/media (depending on what races are coming up and what kind of horses we have running).

SUPERSTITIONS AND DRESS CODE

I DON'T KNOW how other people are, but I'm really superstitious. I look back at pictures to see what I had on when I did well and I go for the same jewelry and shoes. I like to park in the same parking spot. I like to make sure I have my cup of coffee by a certain time. I'll even call one of my clients and say, "I know you are watching at home, but can you put on the suit that you had on the day that you won last time?" If I run a horse and he doesn't perform well, I consider the outfit unlucky. I will never wear it to the races again! I usually wear jeans. It is hard for me to saddle horses with a skirt on.

LIFE AFTER RACING

HORSES THAT PERFORMED well on the track and have a prestigious pedigree are usually sent to finish their careers in the breeding shed, in the hope that they will pass on their superior speed and racing abilities.

HELPFUL HINT

Since speed is often passed down from one generation to the next, breeders and owners will likely place their faith (and money) on the stallions and mares that enjoyed a profitable career at the track.

When a mare reaches maturity and is ready to breed, her owner will pay what's called a stud fee to the owner of the stallion with whom she'll breed. The stallion's owner only gets paid if the mare actually gets pregnant and produces a live foal.

HELPFUL HINT

A "nick" describes the breeding of two bloodlines that produce "better than average results."

In theory, a very busy mare can be bred every year and may produce a dozen or more foals in her lifetime; usually, however, not all of them have the soundness and the talent to race. A busy stallion may sire as many as 100 foals a year and have dozens of his offspring racing at the same track.

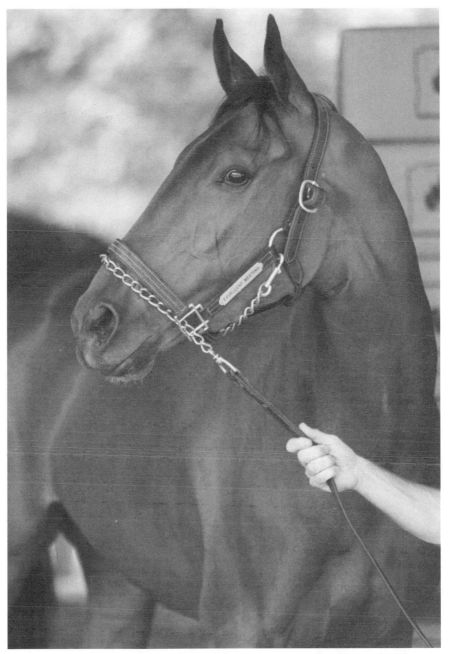

Horses that have performed well on the racetrack are usually sent to the breeding shed.

On March 11, 1943, the 26-year-old Man o' War was retired from a very busy and profitable stud career. He sired 350 foals whose earnings totaled $3 million.

BETTING WINDOW

When you're looking at the *Daily Racing Form*, look at the sires and dams of the horses entered. You'll notice many more recognizable sire names since stallions sire many foals a year.

Exploring Various Racetracks and Race Classifications

6

What Types of Races Are There?

RACING SECRETARIES CONSTRUCT races of all types. There are races for sprint and route horses, experienced and inexperienced, males and females, dirt or grass specialists, etc. The quality of horses usually differs from one race to the next and from one track to another. It is the responsibility of owners and trainers to find the best races for their horses. Some races have weight and age restrictions, claiming prices (tags), and extra entry fees for stakes events. Finding the right race—a spot in which a horse can win—is the ultimate challenge for the horse's connections.

CLAIMING RACES

THE HORSES ENTERED in claiming races are available for purchase at a set price designated by the racing secretary. These prices are published in *Daily Racing Form*. The majority of races in the United States are claiming races. If you go to the track, you'll almost always

have several claiming races scheduled for that day. Since every horse in the race is eligible to be claimed, a trainer or owner won't enter a horse unless he is willing to risk losing him to another owner.

During the 1800's, a common type of horse race was the "selling race." A selling race stipulated that the winning horse could be auctioned off to the highest bidder immediately following the race. This practice (the precursor to claiming races) attempted to keep owners honest by encouraging them not to enter their horses in races where the entry price was too low.

While the selling race did keep some owners honest, others abused the system by purposely having their horses finish second. By finishing second, the horse wouldn't be auctioned off, but would still earn a portion of the prize money. Eventually, the system evolved into what is now the modern claiming race—requiring a potential horse buyer to make a commitment to purchase a horse (any horse in the field) before the race begins.

John Henry was one of the most fascinating rags-to-riches stories of Thoroughbred racing. Although he once raced for purses as low as $2,400, John Henry would later go on to earn Horse of the Year titles in 1981 and 1984 while banking $6 million.

DON'T THINK THAT while enjoying a day at the races you can just plunk down thousands of dollars on a $4,000 claiming race and become the proud owner of a Thoroughbred. Although all the horses in a claiming race are for sale, not everybody is allowed to purchase one. State racing commissions have guidelines on claiming a horse. Every state has its own rules, but for the most part, only owners or trainers who already have at least one horse at that racetrack can participate. So, if you want to claim a horse, you should first familiarize yourself with the state guidelines, acquire an owner's license (or, if necessary, a special claiming license), and then hire a trainer to guide you through the process.

Some horses rise from the claiming ranks to accomplish great things on the racetrack. John Henry was one of those horses. He was sold as a yearling for $1,100, changed hands several more times, and could have been claimed for $20,000. Eventually he was sold for $25,000 and tried on the turf, where he really started to excel. In 1981, at age 6, he was voted Horse of the Year (which was unusual but not unprecedented). He was hampered by injuries during the next two years, but at the age of 9, he won the Arlington Million in Chicago, and the Horse of the Year title, for a second time. John Henry earned more than $6 million during his career.

WHAT HAPPENS DURING A CLAIMING RACE?

AN OWNER DROPS his claim into a claiming box at least 10 minutes before post time. Assuming there's only one claimant (if more than one, lots are drawn to determine the owner), he will own the horse he claimed as soon as the race begins. Even if the horse sustains a career-ending injury, the claimant still owns the horse and is required to pay the specified amount. If that particular horse wins the race, however, the original owner (not the claimant) collects the prize money.

Just because an owner enters a horse in a claming race it doesn't mean that the horse isn't a good horse. Claiming races can range from $1,500 to $100,000, depending on the racing circuit. The average claiming range also depends on the track location. For example, $20,000 to $30,000 claiming races are the most common at tracks in New York. In other regions, however, $5,000 to $10,000 claiming races may be the most common.

THE MAIDEN RACE

A MAIDEN RACE doesn't refer to unwed females. It refers to horses (male or female) that have never won a race. These types of races are for horses that are just getting started with their racing careers. Almost every horse makes its racing debut at age 2 or 3 in either a "maiden claiming" or "maiden special weight" event. Unlike maiden claiming races, which usually feature horses of modest quality, maiden special weight events may include potential champions. Maiden special weight races are for horses that are considered too valuable by their owners and trainers to be entered in maiden claimers. In a maiden special weight race, each horse is assigned the same, or "special," weight.

Northeast-based trainer Linda Rice has established a great reputation for preparing young 2-year-olds for their debuts at the racetrack.

Since every horse begins its racing career in a maiden race, it's almost impossible to know which horse has the greatest chance of winning. Many bettors avoid playing maiden races entirely because of the difficulty in handicapping them. Sometimes, you'll witness the debut of the next great racing star and other times you'll witness a bunch of duds. A trainer's record with maidens is a good indication of how a horse will run. For example, some trainers, such as Linda Rice, have a high win percentage with maiden first-time starters. Other trainers, such as Nick Zito, have a low win ratio with juveniles and take more time conditioning, training, and bringing along their younger stock.

Some trainers, such as Nick Zito, take more time conditioning and training their younger stock.

Zippy Chippy holds one of the longest losing streaks in the history of Thoroughbred racing. "Chippy" racked up no wins in 89 races. His poor performances on the track were legendary. He was eventually banned from racing and retired a lifetime maiden.

BETTING WINDOW

If you want to bet on a maiden race, but have no clue what to look for, check out the horse's breeding lines, recent workouts, and trainer record. At the major tracks, *Daily Racing Form*'s "A Closer Look" will usually tell you if the horse has any winning siblings and whether he is suited to today's distance and surface. You may also want to examine the horses in the paddock area and choose the one that has the best conformation and is behaving professionally. Also, if a first-time starter is being very heavily bet, the word may be out that this is a horse who can run.

7

Races Designed for Superior Horses

ALLOWANCE RACES OFTEN provide racing opportunities for horses that are too good for claiming races, but not quite ready for stakes or handicap competition. Every type of race is different, however, and some high-priced claiming races can prove more intense than an allowance race. Alternatively, some quality-packed allowance races may prove more competitive than a handicap or stakes race with a weak turnout.

Allowance races sometimes give trainers a break in how much weight their horses have to carry (thus the name "allowance"). You will often see allowance races for horses that have failed to win a designated number of races or a certain amount of money in a specified length of time, or for horses that have not won a certain type of race. For example, if a horse wins a maiden race but has not won another race, he may be entered in an allowance race that states, "for nonwinners of a race other than maiden, claiming, or starter."

After "nonwinners of a race other than," the next advancement level in an allowance race will state, "for nonwinners of two races," then "nonwinners of three races," etc.

HANDICAP RACES

HANDICAP RACES ARE another way for racing secretaries to try to create evenly matched fields. Many stakes and some allowance races are handicaps. Racing secretaries try to evaluate each horse's past performances and assign weights accordingly to even out the field. The best horse in a race is expected to receive the most weight, while the horse considered the least accomplished receives the lightest assignment.

WEIGHT ASSIGNMENTS

One or two pounds added to a horse's saddle may not seem like a big deal. But some people believe it can be the deciding factor in the race result, particularly at long distances. In a nonhandicap stakes race, weights are usually determined by The Jockey Club's Scale of Weights. The chart gives recommended weights for horses based on age and sex, each possible distance, and for different times of the year.

The scale generally follows these guidelines:
- The longer the distance raced, the less weight assigned.
- Females carry less weight than males.
- Weight assignments go up as the season progresses. The rationale behind this guideline is that horses will be older, stronger, and in better shape toward the end of the season.

Weight assignments are printed in the track program and *Daily Racing Form.* Any weight changes for a specific race are announced over the PA system, shown on television monitors around the track, and posted on the tote board.

BETTING WINDOW

In general, trainers prefer that their horses race with less weight. Don't assume, however, that just because a horse happens to carry less weight than another horse, it will automatically hold an advantage. Some horses are assigned lower weights because they haven't been performing up to par.

STAKES RACES

STAKES RACES ATTRACT the best horses and offer the greatest purse money. The purses are increased by the addition of entry fees paid by the owners. Some stakes races have special eligibility requirements. Other stakes require that the owner nominate his horse far in advance. The competition in these types of races is generally very strong, and therefore the horse's weight assignments are fairly even. If a stakes race is open to both male and female horses, some weight adjustments may be made. The scale of weights gives weight breaks to female horses when they run against males, and gives 3-year-olds a concession when they run against older horses. There are also some stakes races with a consistent weight assignment. For example, the Triple Crown races require all colts to carry 126 pounds and fillies 121. In addition, there are also handicap stakes where the racing secretary assigns weight based on a horse's ability.

Every once in a while a horse may compete out of its class level in a stakes race simply because his owner wants to associate with the best horses and trainers in the business. Even within stakes races, a pecking order exists. A stakes race can also be a graded event. These types of races are divided into Grade I, II, and III events. A Grade I is the most prestigious and usually worth the most purse money. Graded stakes races are the most distinguished on the annual racing calendar.

Holy Bull, trained by Warren Croll Jr., was one of the most popular stakes horses of the mid-1990's. This striking gray colt finished his career with 13 victories from 16 starts.

Fun Fact

Horses that run in major stakes events are the most high profile and well known by fans. Holy Bull won 11 stakes races and won Eclipse Awards as champion 3-year-old colt and Horse of the Year. Skip Away won 16 stakes races and retired with $9,616,360 in earnings, second to Cigar in North America.

STEEPLECHASE RACES

A STEEPLECHASE REQUIRES the horses to jump a number of 4 ½-foot fences during the running of the race. These events are always conducted over a significant distance of ground—often two miles or so— and run on a grass (turf) course. Some of the bigger tracks schedule an occasional steeplechase race. A growing number of tracks offer steeplechase events, including Belmont Park, Calder, Churchill Downs, Colonial Downs, Delaware Park, Keeneland, Laurel Park, Monmouth Park, Pimlico Race Course, and Saratoga Race Course. Steeplechase races are betting events and wagering is accepted just as in any other race.

Steeplechase racing is always run on a grass (turf) course and tests a horse's stamina and jumping ability.

The Racecourse Oval
(Horses for Courses)

DISTANCE

MOST AMERICAN THOROUGHBRED racetracks measure one mile in circumference and are oval-shaped. However, a track may range anywhere from one-half mile to 1 ½ miles in distance. Many Thoroughbred tracks also use chutes (extensions of the backstretch or the homestretch) so that all races, no matter where they start or how long they are, finish at the same place. When handicapping a race and choosing what horse to bet on, you should consider the distance of the event, the number of turns, and whether these factors fit your horse's running style. The smaller the circumference of the track, the sharper the turns. Some horses have the skill to run fast and maneuver the turns successfully, while others have trouble and are more proficient on the straightaways.

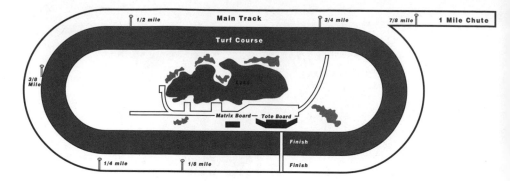

All U.S. racetracks are oval-shaped, but the distance and dimensions of the turns, backstretch and homestretch, differ with each course.

Fun Fact

Belmont Park, which is located in Elmont, New York, is the longest dirt racetrack in the country. It is a 1 ½ mile oval with a 1,097-foot-long stretch. Woodbine, which is located in Ontario, Canada, has the longest grass course in North America. It is 1 ½ miles in length.

Another important factor to consider is the location of the finish line. If you've ever competed in track and field, you can relate to a horse that needs to decrease its momentum around a curve and then has to accelerate for the final push to the finish line. Some horses can accelerate quickly, while others need a few extra yards to get back up to speed. Sharp turns can be problematic for horses that come from behind because it's difficult to pass other horses on a turn. Also, some horses are simply too big and clumsy to race well on sharp turns.

Races generally don't start on turns. When they do, the horses that show good early speed and have drawn inside post positions are usually at an advantage.

Belmont Park is not only the longest dirt track in the country, but is also the site of the Belmont Stakes, the third and final leg of the Triple Crown.

SPRINT RACES

IN ORDER FOR a race to be classified as a sprint it must be seven furlongs or shorter. Six furlongs is one of the most common sprint distances, but you'll also see races of four, 4 ½, five, and 5 ½ furlongs. In some very rare instances, you may even see races scheduled for two and three furlongs. Most of the sprint races that are less than six furlongs are carded for immature 2-year-olds. These juvenile runners are making their racing debuts and still learning the mechanics of the sport. A horse that has good early gate speed will sometimes have an advantage in a sprint race. This is especially true when he is running on a speed-favoring racetrack. A horse's pedigree will also determine whether he is better suited to run in sprint or route races.

ROUTE RACES

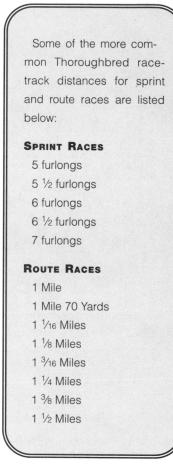

Some of the more common Thoroughbred race-track distances for sprint and route races are listed below:

SPRINT RACES

5 furlongs

5 ½ furlongs

6 furlongs

6 ½ furlongs

7 furlongs

ROUTE RACES

1 Mile

1 Mile 70 Yards

1 $\frac{1}{16}$ Miles

1 $\frac{1}{8}$ Miles

1 $\frac{3}{16}$ Miles

1 $\frac{1}{4}$ Miles

1 $\frac{3}{8}$ Miles

1 $\frac{1}{2}$ Miles

A ROUTE RACE is usually one mile or longer. Route races can be challenging to handicap when a majority of the entrants are attempting the distance for the first time. Although a horse's pedigree can give his trainer some indication of his distance limitations, you can never be completely sure until the horse actually runs the distance. Depending on the racing surface and track bias, a route race can favor speed horses, stalkers (horses who sit three or four lengths from the front of the pack), or come-from-behind runners. A horse with good early gate speed can sometimes steal a route race by building an uncontested early lead in slow time, which allows him to have enough energy left to hold off the runners that close strongly.

Occasionally, you'll find route races that aren't exactly one mile in length; they may be slightly over or under one mile.

HELPFUL HINT

Remember: All tracks are not created equal. Keep in mind that the distances, racing surfaces, embankments, and the location of chutes will vary from place to place.

RACING SURFACES AND TRACK BIAS

DIFFERENT TYPES OF racing surfaces can significantly influence how a particular horse will perform. Racing surfaces can change dramatically from day to day and even from hour to hour, depending on weather conditions. Sometimes these changes produce what is called track bias. Track bias can also be a function of the way the track operators maintain or alter the racing surface. A track bias can favor certain running styles (for example, front-runners versus closers) or specific locations on the track itself. A rail bias may favor runners that are breaking from the first few inside post positions. Recognizing that this type of bias exists, a jockey may try to position his horse toward the inside portion of the track. A rail bias can sometimes develop because the rail is usually the lowest part of the racing surface, making it vulnerable to becoming either hard or soft, depending on the track. Another type of track bias takes the form of a "speed-favoring" track. At some tracks and on some surfaces, horses who get to the front almost always stay there and finish strongly.

"GOOD AFTERNOON LADIES AND GENTLEMEN. TODAY'S TRACK CONDITION... FAST."

Racecourse Oval

At other tracks, horses coming from behind do well. A horse that shows good early speed may be at a distinct disadvantage when attempting to run against a bias that is favoring closers.

In some cases, you can recognize a bias by watching a few of the early races on a particular day's racing card. You can also look at the previous day's results to see what types of runners won and what sections of the track they won from. This can help you determine whether a track bias exists and whether you should adjust your bets accordingly. For example, you may want to ask yourself these questions before heading to the betting windows: Did the front-runners maintain their position throughout the race? Did most of the horses that won stay on the rail, or did they rally from the outside portion of the track? Did the track seem to favor inside or outside post positions?

Don't be too quick to think you've spotted a bias, however. Take into account how the races shaped up, and whether the eventual winners seemed like logical selections. It's possible that the first few races were won by front-runners simply because those horses were the best.

THE DIRT TRACK

DIRT TRACKS ARE designed to be safe in all kinds of weather. But each racing facility's dirt track is "packed" differently, which leaves some faster than others. Following is a list of common racing-surface conditions. The latest track conditions are always posted on the tote board, and on televisions located throughout the inside of the racetrack.

HELPFUL HINT

A dry and loose racing surface that breaks away under a horse's hooves is sometimes said to be *cuppy*. Many horses do not run well on this type of track.

Fast: The footing of the racing surface is at its best. The dirt is relatively dry and evenly manicured.

Firm: A turf course that is in excellent condition. This is equivalent to a fast track on the dirt.

Good: A dirt track or turf course with some moisture in it; not as wet as "muddy" on dirt or "yielding"on turf.

Heavy: The track is worse than muddy.

Muddy: A dirt racing surface that has been soaked by water. This type of track has the tendency to make some horses tire easily. The surface usually favors late-running horses.

Sloppy: A track condition where there is visible water on the surface. A sloppy track can sometimes favor horses with early speed.

Slow: Somewhere between good and muddy.

BETTING WINDOW

Some trainers will use *mud calks*, which are horseshoes designed to provide better traction on muddy surfaces. A bettor should always give extra consideration to horses equipped with mud calks.

Soft: A condition of the turf course that corresponds to "sloppy" on dirt tracks.

Wet-fast: A condition of the dirt track somewhere between "fast" and "good."

Yielding: A rain-softened turf course in which the footing is between "good" and "soft."

HELPFUL HINT

The racing secretary can switch any race from turf to dirt to prevent wear and tear on the grass and to ensure the safety of jockeys and horses.

TURF COURSE (GRASS)

RACING ON THE grass, or turf, is the most popular form of racing throughout the world. In North America, grass races make up only a small portion of each track's racing program. In regions where the weather is sunny and warm year-round, such as Florida and California, turf racing is more prominent. Turf races also make up a significant amount of important stakes races. Most grass races are run at middle to route distances.

Fun Fact Turf horses race over grass courses rather than dirt tracks. Some horses do both, but most perform better on one or the other because of their pedigrees.

The turf course is a lot more sensitive to inclement weather than the main track. If it rains heavily for an extended period of time, most of the scheduled turf races will be switched to the dirt. (Sometimes an important stakes race will be left on the grass, if possible.) The grass will become too slippery for the horses, and the course would likely be damaged if the horses were allowed to run on it. A race that's been taken off the turf usually results in a lot of scratches.

BETTING WINDOW

Many imported grass horses that have run competitively in France (Fra), Great Britain (GB), and Ireland (Ire) also run well in American turf events. Foreign-bred horses will have a two- or three-letter symbol next to their names in *Daily Racing Form*, as indicated above.

THE STARTING GATE

A HORSE UNDERGOES extensive training to help him get used to being loaded into the starting gate, where he must remain calm but alert in a narrow space, flexing his knees and compressing his head and body. As he breaks from the gate, he will either lead with his right or left foreleg. His rear legs start off pushing simultaneously, but then follow the lead of his forelegs. If the horse has started with a left lead, it means that his right rear leg pushes, then his left rear leg, then his right foreleg, then his left foreleg. A horse will change his lead at least once during the running of a race, but it's not uncommon for the jockey to call upon his mount to change leads several times.

A clean break from the starting gate is essential for the horse to get good positioning during the running of the race. Some horses, despite extensive schooling from the gate, will continue to have difficulties well into their racing careers. Some horses have the habit of breaking a few steps slow, which ultimately puts them at a disadvantage right from the start. Other horses dislike loading into the gate. In extreme cases, a horse may have to be backed into the gate or blindfolded before he will enter.

UNDERSTANDING RUNNING STYLES

EACH HORSE HAS a different running style. For betting purposes, it's important to become familiar with the different styles and to compare a horse's style to that of his competitors.

EARLY SPEED

A HORSE THAT usually starts out strong from the gate is known as a front-runner, pacesetter, or speedster. These horses burst out of the starting gate fast and furious. They take the early lead and can either sustain it throughout the running of the race or drop out of contention late. How long an early-speed horse can hold on depends

SPEED CRAZY

on a lot of handicapping variables. The horse's class, post position, conditioning, today's racing surface and distance, and the running styles of the rest of the field all factor into how he will perform. A typical speed horse's running line in the past performances would look something like this:

$$1 \quad 1_2 \quad 1_4 \quad 16^1/_2 \quad 1_9$$

(For more information on reading *Daily Racing Form* past performances, please refer to Chapter 12.)

THE STALKER

In horse terms, a stalker is not someone obsessed with following a certain celebrity. This is the type of runner that sits right behind the speed horses, being conserved for one good late run. Sometimes these horses are said to have tactical speed. If there's no front-runner, a stalking type can sometimes be the pacesetter. If an early duel develops between two or more speed horses at a relatively decent pace, the stalker sometimes has a good advantage. A typical stalker's running line in the past performances might look something like this:

$$5 \quad 4 \; 4^1/_2 \quad 4_2 \quad 31^1/_2 \quad 3^1/_2$$

BETTING WINDOW

If there is only one pacesetter in a race, it might be a good idea to bet on him. Frequently, this early-speed horse can grab the lead, slow the race down, and have enough energy left to hold off the stalkers and closers down the homestretch.

CLOSERS

A HORSE THAT usually comes from far behind and exerts tremendous energy to surge from the back of the field is known as a closer.

These horses can be the riskiest to bet on because they have more traffic problems than the other types of runners, and usually require a quick pace scenario to set up their closing run. The typical past-performance running line of a closer looks like this:

$$2 \quad 10_{12} \quad 8_8 \quad 7_5 \quad 3_{ns}$$

Fun Fact

The horse Silky Sullivan once came from a deficit of 41 lengths to win a race. Sometimes late-rallying horses are called Silky Sullivans.

TOO FAR

JUST RIGHT

TOO SHORT

THE TRACK OWNER USED TO BE A TRAINER

The People
Behind the Scenes

9

The Well-Groomed Horse

The groom is responsible for a large portion of the essential behind-the-scenes work that prepares the Thoroughbred for race day. Listed below are some of these tasks, as described by trainer Hilary Pridham. Pridham is the assistant trainer for Michael Stidham, who trains at Fair Grounds in New Orleans. Stidham is consistently one of the leading trainers in the Midwest.

Hilary came to the United States from England in 1989 and worked as an assistant to Noel P. Hickey at Irish Acres Farm in Ocala, Florida. She was instrumental in helping train 1998 Eclipse Award winner Buck's Boy (champion male turf horse). Hilary has overseen many grooms in her years as a trainer and provides some insight into their routines.

DAILY RESPONSIBILITIES

EACH GROOM IS usually responsible for taking care of three or four horses. The groom's day starts between 4:30 and 6:00 a.m. Some trainers will pay one groom a little extra to get up earlier than the rest of the crew and feed all the horses in the stable. Some of the groom's daily responsibilities include: mucking stalls, taking off the horse's bandages, providing fresh water and hay, and brushing each horse that's assigned to him. Once the brushing is complete, the groom gets the horses ready for any training that's scheduled for that morning. Most racetracks open at 6:00 a.m., but some start operating at 5:30 a.m. (usually in the summer). The horses can arrive at the track for training as early as 6:00 a.m. or as late as 9:00 a.m.

A training chart is provided for each groom. The chart is placed in the middle of the barn and lets them know when to take a horse out. It's the groom's job to know what training "set" the horse goes out in, and to make sure he has the horse ready. The exercise rider brings the groom the horse's saddle and bridle. It's then up to the groom to have his horse brushed off and completely ready for training. It's the trainer's (or assistant trainer's) responsibility to check the horse's legs. It is very helpful, however, if you have an experienced groom who is capable of recognizing any potential physical problems. A groom who can tell you if something is "new" or "different" with the horse's legs and body is always extremely beneficial. The grooms spend more time at the barn than anyone else. They are the individuals who do a lot of the difficult behind-the-scenes work. They establish a real rapport with the horses. It's important to the trainers to have certain horses get along well with certain grooms. If you notice that the groom and horse aren't exactly working well together, you need to make a change.

After the horse gets back from training, it will usually get some kind of therapy. Some horses might get hosed down or have a massage. The grooms don't usually perform this type of work—they simply don't have the time. The groom then brushes the horse again and patches up its legs.

The grooms' normal day ends around noon, but they'll return to the barn at 3:30 p.m. and stay until about 5:00 p.m. During this time frame, they'll clean the stalls again, refill the water tubs, and give the horses their last feed of the day. Sometimes they take the horses out and walk them in the afternoon.

If it's race day, the groom might have a horse stand in ice before its race. They'll also help the trainer put the racing bandages and bridle on. After the race, they're responsible for walking the horse back to its stall. If the horse wins or gets a placement, the groom will accompany the horse into the test barn, where they draw blood and/or urine for testing

LEARNING THE TRADE

MOST GROOMS HAVE been around horses since they were kids. Many of them, however, haven't been around racehorses, so they basically teach each other. It is up to the trainers to teach the grooms how they want things done in their barn. Every establishment is different. Most of what the groom learns is through observation.

Some grooms want to become foreman. Foremen don't groom any particular horse, but they're in charge of all the grooms. One obvious attraction to obtaining the foreman position is that it pays more.

Most horses get fed three or four times a day. For example, a horse might get one feeding at 4:00 a.m., another after training at 11:00 a.m., and again at 5:00 p.m. The foreman's job is to see all the horses at 11:00 a.m. and 5:00 p.m. Ideally, you would like to feed them again, at say 2:00 a.m. or 3:00 a.m., but fewer people are employing night watchmen to perform this task.

SPOTTING THE WELL-GROOMED HORSE

WHEN YOU GO to the paddock area, you'll notice some of the horses have their manes braided. This is strictly a matter of personal preference. Some horses like getting braided, but a lot of them don't.

The groom really needs to know what each horse prefers. The horse's coat is the best indicator of how healthy he is. If the horse's coat looks healthy, and he has a nice shine and glossy appearance, the groom can take some of the credit. But most of the horse's sharp outer physical appearance is the result of a properly balanced diet combined with an adequate exercise and conditioning program. A healthy appearance is usually an indication that a horse is going to run strongly.

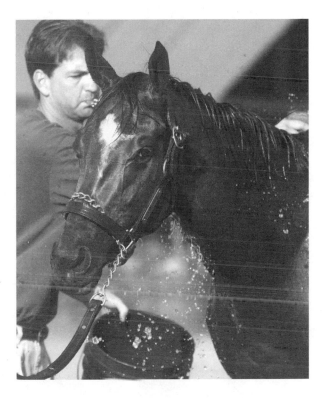

A horse's physical appearance is the result of a properly balanced diet combined with an adequate exercise and conditioning program.

RELATIONSHIPS

A HORSE SPENDS more time with his groom than any other person. If they have a nice relationship, the horse is more relaxed and really able to shine. It's very important to have reliable grooms that really do care about the horses. A horse blossoms when he has someone taking care of him that cares.

Personality compatibility is very important between horses and grooms. Some horses are easy to take care of and others are more difficult. They are very much like people in that they all have different personalities. Most grooms get to the stall and don't say anything. If the trainer notices that the groom is not getting along with his horse, it's his job to give the groom a horse that he does get along with. Most grooms are hard-working and conscientious individuals, and they take a lot of pride in what they do. It becomes an ego thing for them to take care of horses that are happy and doing well at the track. Obviously, they want the better horses. They make more money if the horse wins more money. Depending on the arrangement, they either get a flat bonus or 1 percent of the winnings.

Most trainers and other hands-on barn workers develop a special working relationship with the horses they care for and train. A horse that is happy and comfortable with its surroundings is more likely to perform well on the track.

The Racetrack Veterinarian

10

INTERVIEW WITH DR. TED HILL

eterinarians have important jobs with extremely busy schedules. Some vets work almost exclusively at the track. They make daily visits to inspect, X-ray, and basically prepare each horse for racing. In some cases, outside agencies (or the tracks themselves) employ veterinarians who oversee the health and well-being of the horses.

Dr. Ted Hill has just about seen it all in the course of his many years of involvement in the racing industry. He was the chief veterinarian for the New York Racing Association (NYRA) for 13 years, and has been involved in the sport itself for over 19 years. Hill explains the role of chief veterinarian and some of the other day-to-day responsibilities associated with this challenging position.

BB: *What are the responsibilities of the staff veterinarians?*

Dr. Hill: We have three full-time veterinarians on the NYRA staff. The vets are responsible for giving each horse a thorough exam before each race. [Depending on how many horses are entered on a given day, this could mean that each vet might examine 30 to 40 horses.] We start at about 7:30 a.m. and look for any abnormalities on the horse. The main concern is to protect the horses from further injuring themselves. Despite our concerns, some owners and trainers occasionally protest our decisions. We check the horse's tattoo for identification purposes, the pulse, temperature, eyes, throat, and the flexibility of the limbs to ensure against inflammations.

BB: *How do you determine whether a horse needs to be scratched?*

Dr. Hill: Every owner also has his own private vet look after the day-to-day ailments of his horses. They watch all the warm-ups to make sure no problems exist. A horse may not look good during its initial warm-up or it may get hurt while in the gate. All of these types of developments can lead to a horse being scratched. On the average, one to two horses get scratched from each race.

BB: *What happens if a track veterinarian's opinion regarding a horse's physical differs from that of the owner's vet?*

Dr. Hill: Even though an owner has his own vet examine his horse, it's our responsibility to double-check every horse at the track. In order to check for recurring problems, each vet carries a record of injuries on the horses he examines. This enables us to be somewhat familiar with each and every horse we inspect. Since we have the last word in determining whether or not a horse is allowed to compete, there are, of course, many times when an owner's private vet will be unhappy with our findings. I can only really remember two cases where a horse owner's private vet disputed the findings of the NYRA vets. In both those cases, the other vets backed off, and allowed the ruling of the NYRA veterinarians to stand for fear of further injuring the horse in question.

BB: *What are your responsibilities as chief veterinarian?*

Dr. Hill: As chief vet, my job during a race is to assist any horse that pulls up lame or to respond to any emergency that occurs on or off the track. If a horse pulls up lame or shows any signs of distress during the race, my crew and I will put that horse on a list. The NYRA vets keep an accurate account of this injury list and update it regularly. When the horse's next race comes up, we can then make sure it's now fit to run. I would also put this horse through a workout, and then bring it back to the barn for a cooldown. This is called the postrace check of a horse. The exam becomes part of the horse's permanent record.

BB: *Do you get involved in drug testing?*

Dr. Hill: The NYRA vets don't get involved in drug testing. The horses get drug tested after the race by the state veterinarian at the barn. This is also part of the postrace checkup. Blood and urine are extracted from the favorite in the race and the top three or four finishers of that same race. These blood and urine samples are then sent to the state to be checked for drug usage.

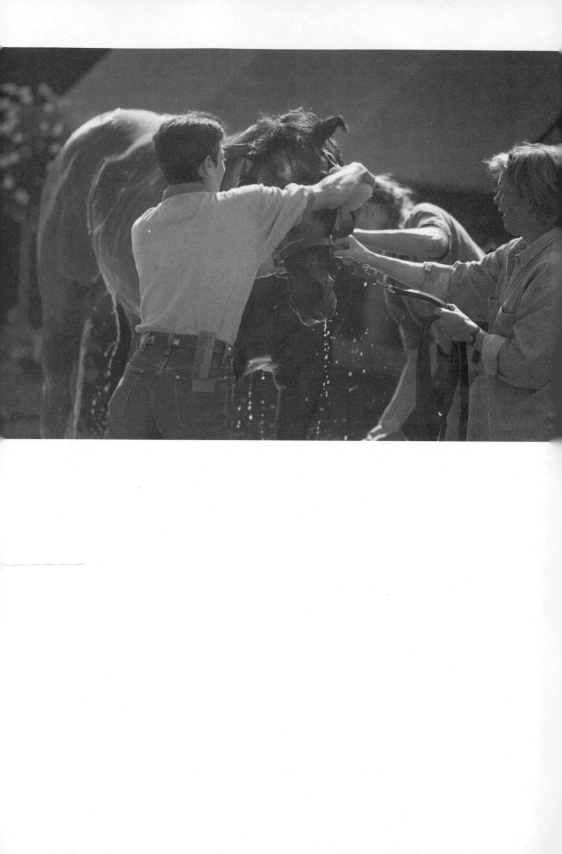

11

The Call of the Races

As you probably guessed, the racetrack announcer calls the races from high above the track grandstand. It's not an easy job. The position requires an individual to have a tremendous memory, a creative personality, and a keen eye. Tom Durkin is one of the best track announcers in the business. Durkin has successfully called races from around the country for 30 years. His many broadcasting accomplishments include the calling of the Kentucky Derby—"the Greatest Two Minutes in Sports"—and the Breeders' Cup. Durkin is renowned in the industry for his quality broadcasts as well as his hard work and preparation.

BB: *How did you first become involved in horse racing?*

TD: I had a friend who was hitchhiking from Chicago to Green Bay (where he attended school). A guy named Marty Helmbrecht picked him up. Marty coordinated fairs in Wisconsin. He told Marty that his friend (me) was an assistant track announcer at Arlington Park, and was sick of playing second fiddle. This was a flat-out lie, since there's no such thing as an assistant track announcer. In actuality, I had never called a race before (only for fun in front of my friends). So, Marty hired me to call races at Fond du Lac County Fair in Wisconsin. Believe it or not, I was calling the races from the back of a pickup truck. A year after college, I worked at odd jobs, but I still knew deep down that someday I wanted to be a track announcer.

When I first started out, I always thought I could get a clerk job at the *Daily Racing Form*. A short time later, I heard about a track-announcer job opening at Florida Downs, which is now known as Tampa Bay Downs. I worked for five years at Florida, moved on to Hialeah, and then on to The Meadowlands. I also started working as a broadcaster on ESPN and NBC. In 1990, I was hired by the

Call of the Races

New York Racing Association (NYRA) to cover all of their tracks (Aqueduct, Belmont, and Saratoga). Also, in 1984, I started calling the Breeders' Cup and this year I called all the Triple Crown races.

BB: *How do you prepare to call a race?*

TD: I mentally prepare for big races (Breeders' Cup, Kentucky Derby, etc.), by doing a little self-hypnosis beforehand. I visualize the race and imagine calling certain things. I also make sure that I'm fully prepared for the type of lingo I'll be using. I keep a book of phrases that I'll run through before a race. These phrases are just fun, interesting ways for me to describe a common race occurrence. If I want to refer to the horse having a slow pace, for example, I may describe it as running nonchalantly, laid-back, lazy, pedestrian, somnambulant, etc.

BB: *What other type of fun phrases do you like to use?*

TD: There are many other common phrases that I frequently use. I like to be prepared to use many different phrases, and I do my best to mix them up. For an extremely fast sprint race, I might describe the pace as feverish, lively, vicious, wicked, mind-boggling, torrid, blitz, throws down the gauntlet, etc. I'll read through these phrases every so often to keep them refreshed in my mind and on the tip of my tongue.

BB: *Is there anything you do between races to prepare for the next event?*

TD: I always critique my own work after every race. I'll write down what I think might have gone wrong or what I believe I can improve upon. I might come to the conclusion that I have to incorporate more words or further improve upon my vocabulary. It's important to have all the elements working correctly. I even give myself a grade after each race.

BB: *Is there any other type of prerace preparation?*

TD: Before the race, I always use the *Daily Racing Form* so that I can familiarize myself with all the races, horses, jockeys, and the race plot.

BB: *What do you mean by race plot?*

TD: I will plot out the horses that are front-runners, and the ones that usually come from far behind to pull out a win in the later stages of a race. I'll also determine what horses are stretching out from a sprint to a route race, and whether or not that will affect their performance. The other important factor to look at is how the jockeys will relate to the horses they are riding. Is the jockey riding a new horse? How has the jockey performed in previous races with a certain horse?

BB: *What other type of information do you utilize from the track program or* Daily Racing Form*?*

TD: It's essential that you read the *Daily Racing Form* prior to the race. I can memorize what horses are scheduled for what races, what owner's colors the horse is wearing, and which jockeys are riding. I'll also try and come up with "cute" and interesting things to say about the horse depending on his name. I'll try and make a point of saying the horse's name, not just his number.

BB: *Since there isn't much of an off-season in racing, what kinds of things do you do on vacation for relaxation?*

TD: Every year my buddies and I rent a place in Tuscany, Italy, and relax by sitting in the beautiful countryside. We read, drink fine wine, and eat great food.

BB: *Do you have any helpful advice for someone who is just starting out in the business or might be considering pursuing a track-announcer career? What steps and preparations should they take?*

TD: Stay out of the business completely because I don't need any more competition! Seriously, the most important thing is to get theater experience. This is important for a few technical reasons. In the theater you get the proper coaching on how to be understood. Speaking correctly is an important part of the job. And the other part of the job is being a performer and getting used to being in front of people. You need to be a performer and have some sort of stage presence. Even if you're a track announcer you have stage presence because you're talking on a public-address system and over the television. There's no real way to learn to call races. You need to find your own style, perhaps by sitting in the grandstand and talking into a tape recorder. The stage presence is definitely the most important thing.

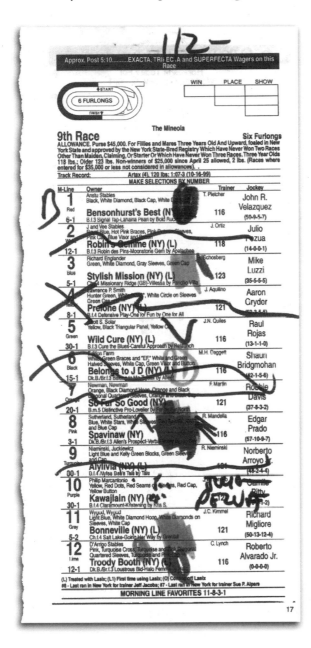

Track announcer Tom Durkin marks up his program to help decipher who's who during the running of the race.

Daily Racing Form:
The Horseplayer's Bible

How to Read
Daily Racing Form
Past Performances

RACING'S INFORMATION HIGHWAY

THIS SECTION IS meant as a primer and a beginner's guide to reading *Daily Racing Form* past performances. It is intended to convey just enough information to make you feel more comfortable about reading the past performances (PP's), and to assist you during your first couple of trips to the track. Evaluating past-performance information and betting on horses can be one of the most exciting and exhilarating parts of the sport. To some, however, the amount of data available can be overwhelming. It is important to remember that the information is there to assist you and not to intimidate you. Have fun with it. Learn some of the basics and pick and choose your own strategies.

You'll often hear people at the track talking about "handicapping." Handicapping simply means using and interpreting information to predict the outcome of a race. Of course, you always have the option of going to the track and just winging it—but if you say

Armed with the *Daily Racing Form*, horse-racing fans can make informed betting decisions.

you're handicapping a race, you'll sound much more sophisticated! Besides, if you learn some of the basic principles involved in handicapping and interpreting past-performance information, you'll stand a better chance of cashing some tickets.

Fun Fact

The *morning line* is the anticipated odds breakdown of a race. The oddsmaker is not predicting the order of finish—just making an educated guess as to how the betting public is going to wager.

Daily Racing Form provides many helpful pieces of information: a list of entered horses, the conditions for each scheduled race, descriptions of each horse, the saddlecloth numbers, and much more. The *Form,* as it is often called, is sold both on- and off-track and has been the premier racing chronicle since 1894. It offers the bettor a wealth of comprehensive data that's not available in any other Thoroughbred-racing publication. The following information is included in every issue of *Daily Racing Form*.

◆ The race conditions for each scheduled event. These are located at the top of the past performances for that race, and include the purse, distance, claiming price (if there is one), age, sex, and any race-record limitations of the horses authorized to be entered.

◆ A complete list of entered horses, usually including the numbers they're going to wear on their saddlecloths. The horses' numbers usually coincide with their positions in the starting gate—but *not* always. Be sure that you're betting on the right horse!

◆ A thorough description of the horse, which includes its age, sex, and color.

◆ The horse's pedigree: sire, dam, and both grandsires.

- The jockey's name, the colors of the racing silks he or she will wear, and the jockey's current record, which includes starts and 1-2-3 finishes.
- The weight to be carried by the horse.
- The name of the trainer and his or her current record.
- The owner's name.
- A list of the wagers offered by each track.
- The morning-line odds and expert handicapping analysis.
- The *past performances* for each horse entered.

HELPFUL HINT

Remember that handicapping is *not* an exact science. Therefore, while handicapping a specific race, you might dissect hundreds of bits of information or maybe just one.

GETTING STARTED

AT THE TRACK, you'll often hear the term *past performances* (PP's). This means exactly what you think. The *Daily Racing Form* contains past-performance information on the horses, jockeys, owners, and trainers. Successful handicappers can interpret this information and use it to help them make informed decisions about the race's most likely outcome.

There is an incredible amount of past-performance data available for every race. Here are a few basics that should have you well on your way to cashing some winning tickets. It might look daunting, but you can learn how to read most of the basic information in a relatively short period of time. Hidden in these lines of tiny print is valuable information on a horse's speed, stamina, and current condition. If evaluated correctly, it just might point you to today's winner!

Almost anything you might want to know about a particular horse is listed in the *Daily Racing Form* past performances. The past-performance charts are divided by race, with one set of PP's for each race. Below is a breakdown of the traditional information provided in the past performances, and how they should be utilized. Please refer to the past-performance line printed below for a clearer explanation.

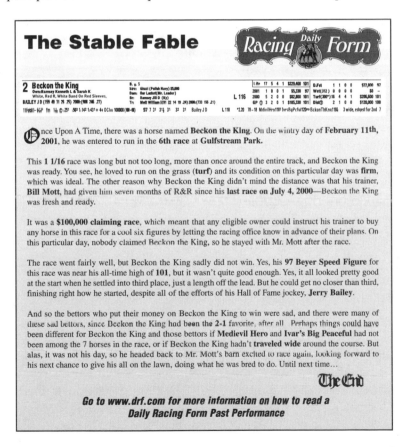

The Stable Fable

Racing Daily Form

Once Upon A Time, there was a horse named **Beckon the King**. On the wintry day of **February 11th, 2001**, he was entered to run in the **6th race** at Gulfstream Park.

This **1 1/16** race was long but not too long, more than once around the entire track, and Beckon the King was ready. You see, he loved to run on the grass (**turf**) and its condition on this particular day was **firm**, which was ideal. The other reason why Beckon the King didn't mind the distance was that his trainer, **Bill Mott**, had given him seven months of R&R since his **last race on July 4, 2000**—Beckon the King was fresh and ready.

It was a **$100,000 claiming race**, which meant that any eligible owner could instruct his trainer to buy any horse in this race for a cool six figures by letting the racing office know in advance of their plans. On this particular day, nobody claimed Beckon the King, so he stayed with Mr. Mott after the race.

The race went fairly well, but Beckon the King sadly did not win. Yes, his **97 Beyer Speed Figure** for this race was near his all-time high of **101**, but it wasn't quite good enough. Yes, it all looked pretty good at the start when he settled into third place, just a length off the lead. But he could get no closer than third, finishing right how he started, despite all of the efforts of his Hall of Fame jockey, **Jerry Bailey**.

And so the bettors who put their money on Beckon the King to win were sad, and there were many of these sad bettors, since Beckon the King had been the **2-1** favorite, after all. Perhaps things could have been different for Beckon the King and those bettors if **Medievil Hero** and **Ivar's Big Peaceful** had not been among the 7 horses in the race, or if Beckon the King hadn't **traveled wide** around the course. But alas, it was not his day, so he headed back to Mr. Mott's barn excited to race again, looking forward to his next chance to give his all on the lawn, doing what he was bred to do. Until next time...

The End

Go to www.drf.com for more information on how to read a Daily Racing Form Past Performance

THE RACE

THE MOST IMPORTANT part of the past performances is the series of lines describing each horse's previous races. It's essential that you learn how to read one of these lines. A typical line reading from left to right would look something like this:

> **1Apr01- 6 Aqu my 6F :23 :46 :58 1:10 4⇑ Clm 35000**

At first the numbers and symbols might appear very confusing, but if you break down each number and symbol individually, it's really not difficult to comprehend.

The date of the horse's last race:
(appears on the left directly under the horse's name)
1Apr01 - The 1st of April 2001.

Race number:
(appears to the right of the horse's last race)
6Aqu - Represents the sixth race at Aqueduct.

Track condition:
(appears to the right of the racetrack and race number)
my - Indicates a muddy track.

Distance:
(appears to the right of the track condition)
6F - The distance was six furlongs.

Fractional times:
(appears to the right of the race distance)
:23 :46 :58 1:10 - The fractions are usually given for the leader's time after the first quarter-mile (:23), then the leader's time after a half-mile (:46), the stretch [in this case, about five furlongs] (:58), and the finish (1:10).

Class of the race:

Includes claiming price, stakes, and restrictions by age, sex, and class. (appears to the right of the final time for the race)

4⇑ Clm 35000- This was a claiming race for 4-year-olds and up at a price of $35,000.

All past-performance charts also include a thorough breakdown of how a horse has performed in its career. This breakdown includes the number of starts, 1-2-3 finishes, and the horse's earnings for the current year and its entire lifetime career. It also indicates how the horse has performed at the track and surface it is running on today. A horse's racing record might look something like this:

A. | Life 22 4 2 6 $135,197 |

B. | 2001 4 0 0 3 $14,850 |

C. | 2000 15 3 2 2 $88,365 |

D. | Aqu 6 1 0 1 $26,390 |

Box A indicates that this horse has made 22 starts in its lifetime, has won 4 times, finished second twice, run third 6 times, and has earned $135,197 for its entire career. Box B is its record for the current year. The horse has started 4 times, finished first and second zero times, and third three times. He has earned $14,850 for 2001. In the year 2000, represented in Box C, this horse ran 15 times, finished first 3 times, second twice, and third twice. His 2000 earnings were $88,365. Box D indicates the horse's record over today's track. In this example the track is Aqueduct (Aqu). This horse has made 6 starts over the track, finished first once, second zero times, and third once. He has earned $26,390 at Aqueduct. *Daily Racing Form* also adds the horse's record over different distances and surfaces. That information is illustrated on page 97.

JOCKEY AND TRAINER STATISTICS

SUMMARIES OF JOCKEY and trainer starts and finishes, plus figures that indicate winning percentages, are included. A jockey or trainer that wins 15 percent of his or her total starts is considered reliable and reasonably talented. Obviously, the higher the win percentage, the better the jockey and trainer. For most races, you'll see two sets of numbers. The first set is the jockey's percentage for the current race meet, and the second figure is his complete percentage for the year to date. The jockey and trainer statistics would look something like this:

A. | Bailey J D (79 20 12 13 .25) 2001: (432 105 .24)

B. | Tr: Mott William I (40 7 5 6 .18) 2001: (348 66 .19)

Box A shows that J. D. (Jerry) Bailey has ridden in 79 races at the current meet, winning 20 times, finishing second 12 times, and third 13 times. He's won 25 percent of his races. In 2001, Bailey has been in 432 races and has won 105 times, for a win percentage of 24 percent. In Box B, trainer William Mott has saddled 40 horses at the current meet, with 7 winners, 5 second-place finishes, and 6 thirds. His runners have won 18 percent of their races at this track. To this point in 2001, Mott has started 348 horses and won 66 times, for a 19 percent win percentage for the year.

Daily Racing Form also prints expanded jockey and trainer percentages elsewhere in the publication. One of the more popular sections among this detailed information is a list of the profitable trainer and jockey combinations for a specific track. Trainers have their favorite riders, and it is always a good idea to check and see how the jockey-trainer teams have been performing on your local circuit. This extended list also shows how the jockeys and trainers have performed in sprint and route races, grass and dirt events, and their percentages with race favorites.

EVALUATING THE RUNNING LINE

| 79 8 7 7₆ 53 ¼ 4 1 ½ 2 ₙₖ Vega H L 117 fb 2.00 81-16 |

79 8 7 7_6 $53\frac{1}{4}$ 4 1 $\frac{1}{2}$ 2 nk **Vega H L 117 fb 2.00 81-16**

THE NEXT NOTATION (**79**) is the *Beyer Speed Figure,* followed by the horse's running line. Andrew Beyer, who is a well-known columnist for the *Washington Post* and an expert handicapper, created the Beyer Speed Figures. They appear exclusively in *Daily Racing Form* and are one of the most popular pieces of handicapping information available. Each figure is designed to quantify the quality of speed shown by a horse in a specific race. It takes into account not only the time of the race, but the distance the horse finished behind, and the track biases and conditions for that day. The higher the Beyer figure, the better the performance. One easy handicapping tip is to look for the horse or horses that have earned the highest Beyer figures in their most recent race or races.

In the above running line (reading from left to right), it's easy to see that the horse broke from post position 8. He jumped out to a slow start in seventh place (7), maintained that position after the first quarter (7_6), moved up to fifth at the half-mile pole (5_3 ¼), was fourth in midstretch (4_1 ½), and finished strongly to miss by a neck in second place (2_{nk}). The smaller number next to each racing position shows his distance in lengths behind the horse in front of him. A horse that shows dramatic improvement in its most recent race might be rounding into top form and worth following up in its next start.

Jockey Harry Vega (as indicated next to the horse's finishing position) rode this horse in this race. The horse received the medication

Lasix (L) (see Chapter 13) prior to the race, and he carried 117 pounds. The (fb) symbol indicates that he was running with front bandages and with blinkers. The next number indicates the horse's betting odds. This horse started the race at odds of 2-1. The next number (81-16) is another speed figure printed in *Daily Racing Form*. This figure is considered by many to offer an inferior assessment of the speed of the race, but was used quite regularly before the introduction of Beyer Speed Figures in April 1992. The first half of the double figure (81) represents the horse's time in relation to the track record (which would be indicated by 100). The second number (16) represents the track variant for the day. Some handicappers add the two numbers together to get a base speed figure. Most educated racing fans, however, ignore this second speed figure altogether, and agree that the Beyer Speed Figures are the more accurate and reliable of the two. It's strictly a matter of personal preference.

The final third of the horse's past-performance line might look something like this:

Queen's Lite 120 2 ¼ There's Trouble 115 ½ Bacara 120 3 ¾ Game finish for 2nd 10

The three names indicate the first three horses in order of finish. Each name is followed by the weight the horse carried, and then by the number of lengths back to the next finisher. The comment that follows gives a brief description as to how the horse performed. By examining the chart caller's comment ("Game finish for 2nd"), we can see that the horse closed strongly and determinedly in the stretch. (Complete racing charts from previous racing dates are available in the back of each *Daily Racing Form,* and through a *Daily Racing Form* weekly publication called *DRF Simulcast Weekly*). The last number on the page (10) shows the number of horses in the race. A second-place finish in a field of 10 is not too shabby, and should be considered a decent effort from a handicapper's perspective.

A horse that encountered significant trouble during the running of a race might be worth betting in his next start. This type of handicapping is known as trip handicapping, and is used by many experienced racing fans. Among the comments listed to the right of the running line that might indicate the horse's performance was better than it seemed are: *blocked, checked, impeded, squeezed start, taken up,* and *wide.*

PUTTING IT ALL TOGETHER

As you can see, there are many numbers and symbols included in the past performances. Hopefully, these explanations will give you a better understanding of what it all means and how you might use the information in making your selections. It's important to remember that there's plenty of time to keep learning. Even the expert handicappers that make selections in *Daily Racing Form* and local newspapers continue to implement new strategies in their handicapping procedures. Having your own opinion and making your own race selections is what makes the game fun and exciting!

13

The Well-Equipped Thoroughbred

JUST AS THE right running shoes can make all the difference for a track star or the right bat can affect a baseball player's batting average, the right equipment can improve a horse's performance at the track. Trainers will often tinker with different types of equipment until they discover exactly what works best for each horse. Let's start from the top . . . the horse's head.

BLINKERS

CUP-SHAPED DEVICES designed to limit a horse's vision are known as blinkers. Blinkers come in a few different shapes. The cups may be less than an inch wide, limiting the horse's view only slightly, or they may be a couple inches or more, allowing the horse to see only directly in front of him. Blinkers may be used on just one eye or on both. These plastic or leather cups are fastened to the back edges of eyeholes that are cut into a hood that fits over the horse's head. The cups restrict the horse's peripheral vision. A horse sometimes requires blinkers to prevent him from swerving into other horses. Blinkers are also used on horses that get nervous or intimidated by the sight of their competitors running beside them, or become jittery and distracted by the sight of racing fans. A trainer often adds blinkers in the hope that by eliminating distractions, they will help the horse "focus" on the race and show more early speed.

A horse that adds blinkers for the first time will usually show more early speed and stay more focused while running. Blinkers also help to alleviate racetrack distractions that may intimidate a nervous horse and affect its performance.

BETTING WINDOW

The racing fan can look at the *Daily Racing Form* to see if a horse is wearing blinkers for the first time, or how that horse has performed in the past with blinkers. Based on this information, a handicapper can determine whether a horse is likely to run better or worse with the addition or removal of blinkers.

SHADOW ROLL

A SHADOW ROLL is usually made of sheepskin and placed over the bridge of a horse's nose to prevent him from seeing shadows on the track. These shadows can sometimes distract a horse and cause him to jump or alter his path during the running of a race, which is likely to cost him valuable lengths. Shadow rolls are especially helpful during night racing, when horses are more likely to see and jump their own shadows. The use of a shadow roll is not reported in the racing program. It is up to the racing fan to recognize whether a horse is equipped with one. If a horse has a habitual problem of jumping shadows, you may want to take special notice when this piece of equipment is first added. The shadow roll, however, is not one of the most important pieces of equipment and rarely is given much consideration from a bettor's perspective.

TONGUE TIE/STRAP

MANY HORSES WEAR tongue ties, which are strips of clothlike material that hold the tongue securely to the lower jaw and prevent the horse from choking on his tongue while racing or working out. On rare occasion, a jockey will be seen pulling up a horse that has "swallowed his tongue" during the running of a race. The horse's air passage becomes partially clogged by the tongue, which ultimately forces him to slow down and stop running. The cloth strip keeps the tongue from slipping back. A tongue tie may also be used to keep the horse from getting his tongue over the bit, thus interfering with the jockey's control. Although the device sounds uncomfortable, most horses don't mind the tongue tie. It is a common and necessary piece of equipment.

THE BRIDLE

THE BRIDLE IS a piece of equipment that adjusts to the horse's head and is used to attach the bit and the reins.

BIT

A BIT IS a metal bar that fits in the horse's mouth and attaches to the bridle. The jockey uses the bit to exercise control over the horse.

SADDLE

THE SADDLE LIES on the horse's back, and in itself, weighs less than two pounds. Horse races, however, have specific weight requirements, which means that sometimes additional weight is added to the saddle to make up the difference. Depending on the weight of the jockey prior to the race, lead weights might be inserted into the sides of the saddle to fulfill these requirements.

SHOES

IT IS NO surprise that the correct shoes are important for the horse. Thoroughbreds run in what are called racing plates, which are made of aluminum and are extremely light. When the track comes up muddy, some trainers may then decide to race their horses with *mud caulks* or *stickers*. Mud caulks look and perform like a pair of cleats, and are designed to prevent slipping and sliding over the racing surface. The decision to use mud caulks is made by the trainer on race day. These new shoes must be put on shortly before post time.

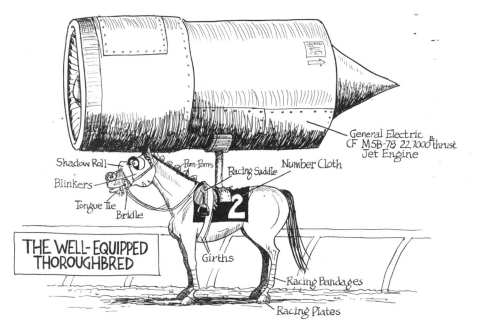

Shadow Roll
Blinkers
Tongue Tie
Bridle
Pom-Poms
Racing Saddle
Number Cloth
General Electric CF M5B-78 22,7000 lb thrust Jet Engine
Girths
Racing Bandages
Racing Plates

THE WELL-EQUIPPED THOROUGHBRED

LASIX AND BUTAZOLIDIN

LASIX IS A BRAND name for furosemide. It is used to reduce bleeding from the lungs when capillaries rupture. The medication diminishes pressure on the capillaries by acting as a diuretic. Horses frequently show significant improvement with the addition of Lasix, which has undoubtedly led to its widespread use in the United States. The notation for Lasix in *Daily Racing Form* or the track program is the symbol *L*. The symbol *L1* is a special notation for first-time Lasix users.

BETTING WINDOW

Lasix is often said to be most important when a horse is using it for the first time. Since the horse's breathing and energy levels are improved, he'll often respond with a much better effort than in his previous, non-Lasix races.

Butazolidin is the trade name for phenylbutazone. Bute, as it is often called, is an anti-inflammatory drug, similar to aspirin for humans, which is used to treat inflammation and thereby reduce pain in those animals suffering from minor orthopedic injuries. It is legal for race day in most states. Unlike Lasix, Butazolidin does *not* have a direct link to improving a horse's performance. The medication is widely used to treat the normal types of athletic injuries that horses sustain in training and racing. The symbol *B* listed next to a horse's name in the track program or *Daily Racing Form* indicates that it is running on Bute.

14

Expert Handicapping Tips

*T*op Southern California rac-ing analyst Brad Free dis-cusses his strategies for helping the novice horse-racing fan. Free is employed by Daily Racing Form and is assigned to handicap each day's race card. He also con-tributes articles and columns about the sport.

Daily Racing Form handicapper
Brad Free.

WHERE TO START

As the Southern California handicapper, I'm required to handicap many races in a very short amount of time. Evaluating the *Daily Racing Form* is kind of like being a detective. You have all the evidence right in front of you, but you only have 15 or 20 minutes to unravel a case. You have to know what you're looking for. The entries are drawn on Wednesday for a Friday racing card. So, I'll know which horses are running about 48 hours ahead of time. The first thing I do is eliminate horses that have no chance. I can usually do that by looking at class and condition. I'm familiar with the entire population of Southern California horses, and I already know each horse's preferences. I can look at a race and usually tell the top contenders just by looking at their names.

I also look at the conditions of the race, the distance, class level, and what surface they're running on. I'll then go through the elimination process and remove horses that have no shot. Once that's completed, I see how the rest of the horses stack up in similar situations. I'll try to determine how the race will be run and if a type of running style will have a distinct advantage. In other words, I'll look to see if there is one front-runner in the race who might lead the field from wire to wire or if there are six front-runners in that same race, which would likely set things up for a closer.

At that point, I'll look at speed figures (which a lot of people use exclusive of other variables). Of the remaining horses, I will look to see if they've been competitive at this level, have finished in the top half of the field, and if they've raced in the top half of the field before tiring. There are other things to consider as well. Trip handicapping (locating horses that have had trouble in their last start) is another popular method of selecting horses. There are a lot of ways to utilize trip handicapping. One way is to combine a horse's pace and speed figures in relation to the type of trip he had. It's important to remember that things that might show up in the past-performance data could suggest that a horse is much better or worse than his last race indicates.

Once I have my selections, I write my analysis for each race. My analysis is an explanation as to why these horses are my top picks.

As a handicapper, my job is not only to give the readers my top three selections, but also to explain rational reasons for them.

MAIDEN RACES

MAIDEN RACES ARE a whole different ball game. These types of races baffle a lot of people. Some people will tell novices not to bother betting a maiden race, but I think that's poor advice. I believe maiden races are easier to handicap than other races because there are not as many variables to consider. In most maiden races, there's usually a bunch of horses that have never run before. If today is a horse's first race, you can evaluate his workouts, trainer, jockey, and pedigree.

LOOK TO THE EXPERTS

AS A NOVICE handicapper, one of the first things I'd do is look at what an "expert" has to say. There are knowledgeable handicappers everywhere, and it's a good idea to start by looking at their columns. You can look to the experts for advice, but that doesn't mean you have to agree with them. The expert might have a reason for liking a horse, but that same reason might be why you dislike that same horse.

FORM HANDICAPPING

THE MOST IMPORTANT handicapping advice for the novice is to start simple. I usually suggest starting with form handicapping. Form handicapping involves looking at a horse that is in form (ran reasonably well in his last or next-to-last race), and running under conditions that satisfy his or her preferences, such as the right class, distance, and surface.

TRAINERS AND JOCKEYS

THE BACKING OF winning trainers and jockeys at your local track are good bets. And, if there were a question as to which one to consider more, I'd weigh the trainer over the jockey. This is especially true in Southern California, where any one of 10 jockeys is interchangeable with the others. The Southern California jockey colony is one of the best out there.

POSITIONING COUNTS

I ALWAYS LOOK for horses that race in the first half of the field during the early part of the race. If there was an eight-horse field, I would insist that a horse's typical running style have him positioned no farther back than fourth place. If a horse is coming from sixth, seventh, or eighth in the early going, he is not going to get there most of the time. The horses with contending speed are the ones that typically win most of the races. There are also many horses that have a tendency to finish second more often than they win. By looking at a horse's lifetime record in its past-performance box, you can easily discover if he qualifies as one of these types. For example, a horse might have started 20 times, but only won twice and finished second six times. These types of horses are often best to avoid.

BETTING ON FAVORITES

THE NOVICE SHOULD not waste time on longshots. I would not recommend betting on anything over 9-1 odds. Betting on longshots is like investing in a penny stock. The novice investor or handicapper is not going to be able to determine if a penny stock has a decent chance at increasing value. Despite popular belief, it's fine to bet on the favorite. You are not going to get rich, but if you look at a race and you settle on a horse that everybody else likes, that's fine. Go ahead and make a bet. Have yourself some fun by watching your horse run and win.

After the race is over, I would advise the novice to go back and look at the past performances of the horse that won and the horse who finished second. I always do that after the race. I'll go back and see whether there was something about the winner that I missed. Part of my job is to continually educate myself on these horses. There is plenty of time between races to do this type of analysis. In fact, one of the criticisms of horse racing is that there is too much time between races. To me, I love the standard half-hour between races. This extra time allows you to watch the replay of the previous race, take a look at the past performances for the next race, and spend another 10 to 15 minutes determining how you are going to bet the upcoming race. I think the amount of time between races is done deliberately, and it makes the racetrack experience much more enjoyable.

A horse's physical appearance and attitude can determine how it will run today. A horse that is sweating profusely or acting up during the post parade is sometimes a bad bet because he's exerting too much pre-race energy.

Expert Handicapping Tips

BODY LANGUAGE

IF YOU WERE at the track, I'd suggest looking at the horses in the paddock before the race. If you don't get to the paddock, you can still watch them on the racetrack. You don't necessarily have to get out of your seat in the grandstand to go look at the horses. Instead, pay attention to what they look like when they come out on the track for the post parade. You don't have to be an expert to analyze body language. If a horse comes out looking like he went through a car wash, he has probably already expended a lot of energy. If that horse was your first choice and he comes out on the track looking that bad, you might want to go to Plan B.

PLACING BETS

IF YOU'RE A novice, I'd only bet to win. I wouldn't bother betting to place or show or any type of exotic bet. I'd keep it as simple as possible. Some people suggest that handicappers wait until the last minute to place a bet. As a beginner, I wouldn't recommend doing so, as it may cause you to get completely tripped up. If you make up your mind 15 minutes before post time, go ahead and bet. If you do bet early, however, you must be willing to go back and cancel your ticket if the need arises. Many people don't realize that you can cancel a ticket anytime before the race begins. If the horse comes out on the track and does not meet your criteria appearance-wise, you can always go back and cancel your bet. Or, if the horse comes out on the track and dumps his jockey and runs off, you can go back and cash your ticket in. It's okay to bet early, but don't be locked in to thinking that just because you've got your ticket in hand you can't go back and cancel it. It is also okay to sit out a race. There are plenty of times when I wish I didn't have to make a selection.

FINDING VALUE

IF YOU'RE AN experienced bettor, you are not going to be betting the favorite in every race. If you are taking a chance every now and then, a good win ratio is 20 percent. If you are betting the favorite in every single race, your win percentage is obviously going to be much higher, usually in the 30 percent range. The bottom line is being able to accurately assess a horse's true chance of winning and wagering when the odds on the board are higher than what you think they should be. The name of the game is getting value for your money.

HELPFUL HINT

For more information, Brad Free suggests picking up copies of *The Handicapper's Condition Book* (James Quinn), *Modern Pace Handicapping* (Tom Brohamer), *Picking Winners* (Andy Beyer), and a copy of the *Daily Racing Form.*

15

Place Your Bets

HOW TO PLACE A BET

ONCE YOU'VE FIGURED out which horses to bet on, it's important
to know how to place the bet and what kind of wager to
make. Horse racing offers a multitude of betting opportunities that
are relatively easy to learn, and with few exceptions (watch for those
$50 minimum windows!), you can go to any track window and put
down any number of dollars you choose.

For some first-time track visitors, the mere thought of stepping up
to the betting window to make a wager is frightening. The most
important thing to remember is that the tellers are generally very
pleasant, helpful, and patient (assuming there isn't a big line of bettors waiting behind you). Once you think you've learned how to
make a wager, you may want to place the bet well before post time
until you get comfortable with the whole process. The quicker you
get your bet in, the happier the people standing behind you will be.

Once you've decided how much money you're betting and which horses you're betting on, you'll be expected to place your wager in a specific order. That order is as follows:

1. Announce the name of the track that you're betting on.
2. Announce the number of the race you're betting on.
3. Announce the amount of your wager.
4. Announce the type of wager you wish to make.
5. Announce the number of the horse or horses involved in your wager.

So, for example, if you were at Keeneland and wanted to bet two dollars on the number 6 horse to come in first in the fourth race, you'd say: "Keeneland, fourth race, two dollars to win on number six." It's also a good idea to write down your betting numbers on your track program or *Daily Racing Form* so you can refer to them when making the bet. Once you've successfully announced your wager, the clerk will give you a ticket or tickets that include all of your bets. When you receive your tickets, be sure to check them for accuracy. If there is a mistake on your ticket, such as the wrong betting amount, number, racetrack, or race number, the clerk can correct it right on the spot. As long as you notice the mistake prior to the running of the race, you can have the ticket canceled and corrected at any betting window.

Most racetracks offer a couple of different ways to place a bet. You can use a betting machine, better known as a SAM. This is a screen-activated self-service terminal that allows you to place a wager. SAM's are conveniently located throughout the racing facility. All machines accept betting vouchers, which can be purchased at voucher machines or tellered windows. Simply insert the voucher or a winning ticket and follow the easy instructions on the screen. These machines offer a quick and efficient way to place a bet and are very user-friendly, which makes them ideal for the beginner.

PARIMUTUEL SYSTEM

MODERN-DAY HORSE wagering is run by a parimutuel system. In simple terms, payoffs for a horse are determined by how much total money is placed on a race. The money played by all of the bettors is pooled. Therefore, the tracks don't care which horse you bet on because they automatically deduct a small amount off the top and return the rest as a payout. Essentially, you are competing against the guy next to you, not against the track. The track is not losing its own money—the money that is paid out comes from the individuals that are holding losing tickets.

Fun Fact

The auction pools in Paris, France, were referred to as mutuels. When the French brought a new form of gambling to the United States (the system used today), it became known as parimutuel betting.

HOW THE SYSTEM WORKS

THE ODDS ON a horse inform the bettor how much his payoff will be if he bets on that particular horse and he wins. These odds are determined by how much money is bet on each horse in relation to the rest of the field. The odds on the tote board are based on win wagers. They reflect the odds to $1 unless otherwise indicated. It is easy to calculate approximate payoffs. There are a couple of different ways to determine how much you'll make (based on a $2 wager). These methods will only give you an approximate payoff, however, because the odds can change right up to the last few seconds before post time. Every track calculates odds for each horse based on the amount of money in the betting pool. Once the race begins and the betting has closed, the track calculates the final odds on which the payoffs to the winners will be based. Remember: The odds are determined not only by how much is wagered on a specific horse on-track, but also by the combined bets from all other legal betting establishments (including other racetracks and off-track betting venues).

Traditionally, racetrack payoff figures are based on a $2 bet, even though odds are worked out based on $1. The reason for this is that the minimum bet used to be $2. Today, most tracks accept bets of any amount from $1 on up (in whole-dollar amounts). Once you figure out the payoff for $2, you can easily calculate what you'll get for any other amount. If the odds are to "1" (as in 5-1), double the odds and add your $2 wager. For example, a $2 win bet on a 5-1 horse will pay $12 (5 x $2 = $10 + your $2 wager = $12). If the odds are not based on "1" you can mentally adjust them so that they are. For example, odds of 7-2 can be changed to 3 ½-1. You then multiply the first number by 2, add your initial $2 investment to the total, and you have your payoff for a $2 bet, $9.

PAYOFFS (ASSUMING A $2 WAGER)

IF YOU DON'T want to bother with the math calculation, and you're still a little confused by the odds on the tote board, the following chart shows a list of payoffs based on a $2 win ticket for various odds. You may want to make a copy of this chart and take it with you on your next trip to the track.

HELPFUL HINT

The odds are based on the amount of money wagered on a particular horse to win, not to finish second or third.

PAYOFFS ON A $2 WIN BET

Odds	Payoff	Odds	Payoff
1-10	$2.20	7-2	$ 9.00
1-5	$2.40	4-1	$10.00
2-5	$2.80	9-2	$11.00
1-2	$3.00	5-1	$12.00
3-5	$3.20	6-1	$14.00
4-5	$3.60	7-1	$16.00
1-1	$4.00	8-1	$18.00
6-5	$4.40	9-1	$20.00
7-5	$4.80	10-1	$22.00
3-2	$5.00	12-1	$26.00
8-5	$5.20	15-1	$32.00
9-5	$5.80	20-1	$42.00
2-1	$6.00	50-1	$102.00
5-2	$7.00	60-1	$122.00
3-1	$ 8.00	99-1	$200.00

TRACK TAKEOUT AND BREAKAGE

A RACETRACK WITHHOLDS anywhere from 10 to 30 percent of each wagering pool depending on the type of wager. A separate pool is maintained for each kind of bet in each race. This takeout is the combined revenue of the state government, the track, and other governmental or racing entities. The figure varies, depending on how much the individual state is mandated to take. Breakage is the procedure of rounding down payoffs to the next 10- or 20-cent increment. This money is sometimes used to pay off bettors in the minus pool, something that will be explained later in this chapter. The racetrack's percentage goes to pay its operating expenses, which usually include salaries, racetrack upkeep, purse money, etc.

The tote-board provides a wealth of information for the bettor.

Fun Fact

A *minus pool* is one in which there is not enough money to pay back everybody who bet on a horse, plus the track's minimum return of 10 cents on the dollar. A minus pool can sometimes occur when a heavily favored horse wins.

THE TOTE BOARD offers the racing fan a wealth of information. It includes a lot more than the odds for each horse. Depending on the track itself, the amount of data that is provided will vary. Most tote boards include the odds for each horse, results and payoffs of the last race, time of day, the post time for the next race, track condition, dollar amounts for the win, place, and show pools, scratches, equipment changes, and fractional and final times of the current race, although not all of this information is displayed at the same time. The track's race caller also announces some of these things

over the public-address system. The tote board, however, is a much easier way to get this valuable information. If you're busy talking with friends, you may not be tuned in to what is being announced, and you might miss some important information regarding the day's races. The win pools, which affect the horses' odds, and the place and show pools, are monitored and updated by computers. The odds are continuously changing as money is being wagered.

HELPFUL HINT

In betting terms, the phrase "in the money" refers to a horse that finishes first, second, or third in a race.

WHAT TYPES OF BETS ARE THERE?

THERE ARE MANY different kinds of bets, and some can be a little complicated for the novice to comprehend. There is actually a name for the most interesting and sometimes complicated bets. They are appropriately called *exotics*. The beauty of horse racing is that you can make your betting as simple or as complicated as you like. Here is a thorough list of the wagering options available at most racetracks:

Win: You are a winner if your horse wins the race.

Place: If you bet a horse to place and he finishes first or second, you are a winner.

Show: If you bet a horse to show and he finishes first, second, or third, you are a winner.

Across the Board: If you want to bet one horse to win, place, and show, you may simplify the bet by telling the mutuel clerk that you wish to wager, for example, $2 *across the board* on horse number 4. (In this case, you're actually placing three $2 wagers for a total of $6.) If the horse wins, you collect for win, place, and show. If the horse finishes second, you collect for place and show, and if the horse finishes third, you collect for show.

Daily Double: The daily double is one of the oldest and simplest of the exotics. The wager calls for the selection of the winning horses in two designated races. Most racetracks offer a daily double on the first and second races of the day. Sometimes the daily double is placed on the last two races of the day. One of the daily-double races usually features a large field made up of horses that are extremely hard to figure. Maiden-claiming races (which are some of the cheapest races available) are a particular favorite for the first or second race in a double.

"WOULD A 10-2 DAILY DOUBLE
BE OUT OF THE QUESTION?"

Exacta (or Perfecta): An exacta is a wager that calls for you to pick two horses to come in first and second in exact order. Most racetracks take exacta wagering on almost every race. The *box* is a popular betting tactic in exactas. You may box an exacta when you do not strongly prefer one horse to the other. A box allows your two selections to run first and second in either order. For example, an exacta box using the number 4 and number 9 horses consists of two separate bets: the 4 can run first and the 9 can finish second, or the 9 can finish first and the 4 can finish second. This particular exacta box costs $4 based on a $2 wager. You can box as many horses as you like, but the more horses you use, the more combinations are possible, and the more the bet costs. You can also bet a "straight" or "cold" exacta by calling out your horses' numbers in exactly the order you think they'll finish.

Quinella: A *quinella* wager costs you the price of a single bet but takes care of boxing for you. The wager requires you to pick two horses to finish first and second in either order. Although the bet is twice as easy to win as an exacta, it tends to pay about half as much.

Trifecta: You must select the first, second, and third horses in a race, in their exact order of finish. The payoff on a trifecta can be extremely high if a couple of longshots finish in two of the three positions, or if a heavy favorite finishes out of the money. Because a large field offers so many possible combinations in the order of finish, the trifecta is not an easy bet to cash. Like the exacta, you may also box the trifecta.

Superfecta: The superfecta requires you to select the first, second, third, and fourth horses in a race, in their exact order of finish. The payoff on the superfecta is usually even higher than on the trifecta because of its increased difficulty. Like the exacta and triple, you can box the superfecta.

Pick Three: You win by selecting the winners of three designated races. You can select more than one horse in each race, but the cost of your wager will increase. If, for example, you use two horses in the first leg, three in the second, and two in the third, you would spend $24, based on a $2 bet (2 x 3 x 2 = 12 x $2 = $24). The pick three is sometimes called the *daily triple*.

Pick Four- You win by selecting the winners of four designated races. As in the pick three, you can select more than one horse in each race, but the cost of your wager will increase.

Pick Six- It's not an easy task to select the winners of six consecutive races, but the payoff is usually very large, depending on the number of bettors who can correctly select the winning combination. The pick six is usually the largest payoff available at the racetrack. Even when nobody wins, consolation payoffs go to the individuals that correctly picked five or even four winners from the six races. The bulk of the pick-six pool is carried over to the next racing day.

THE COMBINATION WAGER, OR BOX

In races where multiple-horse bets are offered, players may combine several horses to increase their chances of winning. Each additional horse that is added to a ticket, however, raises the cost of it considerably. Listed below are the costs of exacta and trifecta boxes based on a $2 bet.

BETTING WINDOW

A popular exotic bet is known as the *wheel*. In a wheel, a bettor picks one or more "key" horses and places bets around that horse, assuming it will finish in a particular spot. Usually bettors key a horse to win and then wheel other horses in the race in the second and/or third spots.

Exacta Box (Based on $2 per bet)		Trifecta Box ($2 per bet)	
2 Horse Box	$4	3 Horse Box	$12
3 Horse Box	$12	4 Horse Box	$48
4 Horse Box	$24	5 Horse Box	$120
5 Horse Box	$40	6 Horse Box	$240
6 Horse Box	$60	7 Horse Box	$420

HELPFUL HINT

An overlay refers to a horse that will pay a higher price than he appears to warrant based on his past performances. In other words, the public is overlooking a horse you think will perform well. An underlay is the opposite.

Fun Fact

Betting a horse to win, place, or show is called *straight wagering*.

PAY UP!

The Thoroughbred Athlete's Key Personnel

16

A Day in the Life of Hall of Fame Jockey Jerry Bailey

BEHIND THE SCENES WITH JOCKEY JERRY BAILEY

*O*ne of the greatest riders of all time, Jerry Bailey won his fourth Eclipse Award as outstanding jockey of the year in 2000. He previously earned Eclipse Awards in 1995, 1996, and 1997. Inducted into racing's Hall of Fame in 1995, Bailey has had a distinguished racing career that has shown no signs of slowing down. In 1995, he rode the famous Cigar (1995 and 1996 Horse

Hall of Fame jockey Jerry Bailey is one of the most popular and successful riders of all time.

of the Year) to victory in all 10 of his races. In 2001, Bailey hit a major milestone in his career by winning 5,000 races. His dedication and love of the sport of horse racing have made him one of the most popular jockeys in the world. Bailey gives an in-depth look at life as a jockey.

GROWING UP

MY FATHER WAS a dentist who loved going to the races. We lived in El Paso, Texas. Almost every weekend my family would go to Sunland Park in New Mexico, which was about 15 to 20 minutes from our home. Sunland Park was a legalized racetrack that held races every Friday and Saturday night. As my father became more enthusiastic about the game, he began to purchase horses and became an owner. I started hanging around the barns between races and on weekends, which eventually led to walking horses before and after school. I started at the bottom. I first became a groom and later an exercise rider. It wasn't difficult finding jobs. My father, through owning horses, had many outside contacts with trainers.

I never thought I'd become a jockey. I always wanted to be a football player. In fact, I wanted to be a Green Bay Packer. At around age 12, I realized that could never happen because I was too small. At the time, grooming and riding horses was just a good way to make summer money—the alternative being mowing lawns or delivering papers. The horse business was a little more intriguing to me.

BECOMING A JOCKEY

WHEN I REACHED the age that I could get a jockey's license, which is 16 (although I waited until I was 17), I graduated high school and became a proficient exercise rider. I figured that once I turned 17, it would be fun (and I was light enough) to try and become a jockey. Fortunately, I won on the first and second mounts I ever had. The horse's name was Fetch. I rode Fetch on Saturday and again on Sunday. I was hooked. Everyone in my family was surprised that I wanted to become a jockey. My whole family has a medical background, as does my wife, and I was kind of the black sheep. It really wasn't a lifelong goal at the time.

After winning with my first two mounts, you would think it would be easy to get a jockey agent—but it wasn't. Coming from a family with a strong professional background, I don't think anybody took me too seriously. I had to call a friend that I came across during my years of exercising horses to get mounts. He was a good agent but had moved back to Washington. He always said that if I needed an agent I should call him, so I did. None of the local agents in West Texas were interested in representing me. I gave my friend a call and he flew down. After that, I was the leading apprentice and/or leading rider wherever I went for the next year.

I've had several agents since then. Your relationship with your agent is almost like a marriage. As long as things go well, and you get along well, it lasts. Sometimes, at some point, things just don't go right and you end up splitting. The decision is sometimes mutual, but other times it's not.

TRAINING SCHEDULE

YOU HAVE TO be very fit to ride. A lot of people ask me what I do to stay fit. There is not one, two, or three things I could say that would get you absolutely fit for being a jockey other than routine itself. Certainly, exercising horses in the morning helps, but it's not the same as riding a race in the afternoon. Most jockeys, once they start riding full-time, will ride four, five, six, or even seven horses daily. In the Northeast, where we race five or six days a week, there's no need to do anything else to get in shape. Also, there is probably not enough time to do anything else. We don't lift weights because that puts on muscle mass, which puts on weight. It's a delicate balance between staying fit and staying light. You've got to be careful. Maybe 1 percent of the riders actively lift weights in their process of staying fit, and they often have weight problems.

EARLY MORNING

GENERALLY, I RISE around a quarter to six in the morning and I go out to the racetrack. I get to the track around 6:00 or 6:15 a.m. and generally exercise one horse. Sometimes I'll get on two or three horses in the morning. In Saratoga, I ride more because it's much busier.

My only real meal during the day is breakfast, which consists of a cup of coffee and an English muffin. In lieu of an English muffin, I might have a piece of toast or a bagel. In warm months when I sweat a lot, I'll have a breakfast drink consisting of banana, frozen fruit, soy milk, yogurt, and vitamin powder.

When I get to the track to exercise the horses, I'll work the ones that I'll be riding in the future. There are usually two main categories. The first type is a horse that's never run before (2-year-olds that trainers want me to get a feel for), and then there are stakes horses (trainers want a light jockey on them instead of a heavier exercise rider). After I ride a couple of horses, I'll spend a lot of time on PR. A lot of owners and trainers come out in the morning. I'll discuss the races I've ridden for them the previous day, or what I will be riding for them in the future. I probably ride close to 1,000 horses a year. About 600 of them will be ones that I don't ever ride again. On the average, I ride for about 25 trainers and they may have between five to seven different owners. I probably ride for over 100 owners a year. It's a constant flow.

MID-MORNING TO EARLY AFTERNOON

I'M PROBABLY FINISHED at the track around 9:00 or 9:30 a.m. I'll then come back home. I rarely stay at the track all day long. For me, it's a better escape to go home. I would get too sour staying at the track all day. When I get home, I'm like any other person. There are errands to be run, bookkeeping chores to be completed, and other odds and ends.

I'll get back to the track before my first race. If I'm riding in the first or second heat, I'll have to be back to the track by noon. If I don't ride until the fifth or sixth race, I don't have to be there until 2:00 or 3:00 p.m. So, I might play eight or nine holes of golf before I return. Whatever I do, I try to stay active instead of taking a nap.

I definitely don't have any lunch before heading back to the track. I'll eat pieces of fruit throughout the day, but that's it. I keep my energy up by taking lots of vitamins. I don't drink a lot of water. If you have a glass of water, and you have to ride a lightweight, that's a pound. You'll have to go to the steam room and lose it. If I have any lightweights that day, I will have to refrain from drinking too much until after the day is over. But since I had kidney stones, I've raised my riding weight so I can drink more. It's difficult not to think about food during the day. If I keep busy riding horses, however, I tend not to think about being hungry. If I have two or three races off, I definitely think about eating.

RACE TIME

WHEN I GET back to the track, I'll go through the *Daily Racing Form* and handicap the races I'm riding in. I want to see the other horses and jockeys that I'm up against, and what their running styles are in relation to mine. I'm not always familiar with the horse that I'm riding. In the big races, however, I'm usually familiar with each horse's running style. Most of the stakes horses are in the same types of races, and they usually run once a month. But every day there might be a maiden race with 10 fresh faces (horses that have never run before), and you might be on a horse you've never ridden.

If I can't remember a race or I can't decipher what I'm seeing in the *Daily Racing Form,* I'll look at videotapes. We have a TV with a video bank that we can view past races from inside the jockeys' room. I'm familiar with most of the other jockeys riding and I know their styles. By competing with them, you get to know their habits. After handicapping the day's card, it's time to go ride my first race of the day. Before post time we have a 10- to 15-minute prayer service. It's essentially a safety prayer group in which we pray for people who are ailing.

DURING THE RACES

AFTER EACH RACE I change clothes. If I've gotten dirty, my valet will brush off my boots and pants. I change into my new silks for my next race. If I don't have a race coming up, there's plenty of ways to pass the time. There's a pool table and a Ping-Pong table, and TV's are located in the jockeys' recreational lounge. You are not allowed to leave the jockeys' room until you are finished racing. Interviewers will come to you, and security guards will escort you to sign autographs, but you can't leave the room.

All of the jockeys have a pretty good rapport with each other. It's a very unique sport in that it would be like two football teams dressing in the same locker room. Like in anything, there are conflicts in personality, but I would say 95 percent of the time everyone gets along. We have a great deal of respect for each other. You can't hold grudges too long because people can get hurt. I think everyone knows that. Therefore, we try to keep it very professional at all times. It's amazing considering the competition involved. You have guys that get cranky from being deprived of their normal meals and tempers can flare easily.

The first thing we do when we go to the jockeys' room is weigh ourselves to see if we have to do penance in the steam room. In fact, we weigh ourselves all day long. If you still have a lightweight race scheduled, but you want a banana or three or four ounces of water, you try to sustain yourself. Before the race itself, we're also "officially" weighed. You step up on the scale, your valet brings your equipment, and you weigh in with your saddle. If you have to be a couple extra pounds heavier, there are pockets in the saddle that lead can be inserted or you may have to wear weighted pants.

AFTER THE RACE

AFTER THE RACE we're immediately weighed again to make sure we carried the weight assigned, and that no lead fell out or any mistakes were made like switching saddles. It does happen, but it has never happened to me. After my last race, I take a shower and I'm gone usually before the next race runs. When I get home, I always eat dinner. How light I am at the end of the day will dictate my diet. However, my diet doesn't change too much. I eat high carbs and low protein, which includes a lot of pasta, very little sauce, and red meat, chicken, fish, and always water. I don't drink alcohol or soda. I do give myself a little treat once in a while. I love chocolate, which can be a problem for me. I'll stop eating dinner just so I can have a piece of chocolate! My wife really helps me out with the meals. Before I met her, I was the steak-and-potatoes kind of guy. She has really taught me how to eat properly. She cooks real light and she makes desserts with light products, such as skim milk.

I am usually in bed by 10:30 p.m. On my days off, my routine changes very little. I'll still try and play golf every day and eat roughly the same foods. If the weather isn't good, I'll read a book. There are always things to be done indoors, such as making plane reservations, etc.

PERSONAL LIFE

MY SON IS 8 years old. He used to come to the track more often, but he's now into baseball and soccer. It's highly unlikely he'll get into horses as much as I was. In fact, I wasn't into horses until I was 11 or 12. I was into other sports, and so is he. My son is a pretty good athlete.

Being a jockey is probably toughest on my wife because I'm gone from 6:00 in the morning till 6:00 at night. My wife tries to come to the track when her schedule permits. My son has a lot of activities that she has to take him to, so it's not always easy for her to get to the track for every race.

ON THE ROAD

BEING ON THE road for races is not that difficult or different for me. We have homes in all three of the main places I ride—Miami, New York, and upstate New York (Saratoga). The rest of the trips are only one-day trips, other than the Kentucky Derby and the Breeders' Cup. Most of the time I'll stay in the same hotel. My wife and son will almost always go to the Kentucky Derby and Breeders' Cup with me.

VACATIONS

I HAVE THE whole month of December off. So, we'll sometimes take a little vacation. In the spring, there are three weeks between the Florida meets and before the Kentucky Derby. I'll take a little time off then and only work on the weekends.

LIFE AFTER RIDING

I'LL PROBABLY CONTINUE for about another three years. After that, it's hard to say. I might do TV. I wouldn't mind staying involved in the sport, but I would really like to spend some more time with my son. Racing's big days are weekends and holidays, and those are the times I want to spend with my son and my wife. So, it will be hard to be involved in racing if I want those times off.

FAVORITE HORSES

LIKE A DOCTOR trying not to get involved with his patients, I try not to get too attached to my horses because there is such a high rate of turnover. My favorite horse was Cigar. Not only was he the best horse that I've ever ridden, but also he was at a high level for such a long time, which created a good bond between everyone involved. He won 16 races in a row.

Jockey Jerry Bailey and trainer Bill Mott have been an inseparable team on the racetrack for many years. The mighty champion Cigar, piloted by Bailey and conditioned by Mott, accumulated 19 career wins and $9,999,815 in earnings.

Bailey guides Cigar to a handy win in the Grade I Woodward Stakes at Belmont Park.

FAVORITE RACES

I WON THE Kentucky Derby twice and that's very special. The Derby is like the Indianapolis 500 for the race-car driver or the Super Bowl for the football player. But there is a race called the Dubai World Cup at the Nad al Sheba racecourse in the United Arab Emirates of Dubai. Cigar won the inaugural running. This race is high on my list of favorites, because it's more for America than anything else.

OTHER INTERESTS

I STOPPED RIDING for six months and went back to college at my mother's request. I've always been fascinated by numbers. I probably would have been an accountant if I didn't become a jockey.

ODDEST RACES

I'VE EXPERIENCED A few really odd races in my career. Back in 1976, at Arlington Park in Chicago, I was riding in a long route race where the horses broke in front of the stands. When we came around and turned for home, the starting gate was still there! Everyone had to go single file by a small space created by the rail. It was very strange and they discounted the race. At the same track a year later, we were racing on the turf course and someone left the lawn mower on the backstretch! The guy on the lead almost had to stop completely so his horse could go around it.

IMPROVEMENT FOR THE SPORT

I WOULD LIKE to see the jockeys' weight restriction raised. It's been almost the same for the past 100 years, and people are getting bigger. That subject needs to be addressed.

All jockeys have to watch their weight very carefully. I certainly do, even though I'm not one of the heavier guys. There are guys that have a lot bigger weight problems than I do.

Raising the weights would keep your "stars" around longer. There are many excellent riders that leave the profession due to weight problems. It's very unfortunate.

Fun Fact

The Jockey Club is not a group of jockeys who socialize with each other. It is the official registrar of all Thoroughbreds in the United States.

WHAT IS A JOCKEY?

The term jockey used to apply to someone involved in horse-trading. Nowadays, of course, a jockey is the person who rides the horse. Jockeys have a difficult job. They have to be both strong and light, which is a tough combination. Most jockeys weigh about 110 to 112 pounds and average 5 feet 4 inches in height.

Jockeys must have tremendous upper body and lower-body strength. They require quick reflexes and good judgment. They must have the skill and athleticism to maneuver 1,000- to 1,200-pound horses through some very tight quarters. Pound for pound, the jockey is the strongest athlete in the world.

Fun Fact

Every track provides a special steam room for jockeys to sweat off excess weight before a race. This room is called a hot box.

APPRENTICE JOCKEYS

An apprentice jockey is a rider in his first year of racing. The apprentice is given certain weight allowances to make him more competitive and encourage trainers to use him. Apprentice jockeys are often referred to as bug boys. This term came about because of the asterisk placed next to the name of the jockey on the racing program. "Bug boy" is used for both male and female jockeys.

Fun Fact

If an apprentice jockey has only zero to five wins, he will get a 10-pound weight allowance (and three asterisks by his name, called a triple bug boy). If he has between six and 35 wins, he'll only get a seven-pound weight allowance and he'll be called a double bug boy.

A Day in the Life of Trainer Bob Baffert

BEHIND THE SCENES
WITH TRAINER BOB BAFFERT

Three-time Eclipse Award winner Bob Baffert is one of the most talented and colorful Thoroughbred trainers of the modern era. In 1997 and 1998, Baffert won both the Kentucky Derby and the Preakness, first with Silver Charm and then with Real Quiet. Each colt narrowly missed winning the Belmont Stakes, the third and final leg of the Triple Crown. In 2001, Baffert won the Preakness and the Belmont with Point Given.

Year in and year out, Baffert ranks among the country's top trainers in money won, and led that category in 1998, 1999, and 2000. He has not only had tremendous success on American soil, but also is a two-time winner of the Dubai World Cup. The Dubai World Cup, which is held at the Nad al Sheba racecourse in the United Arab Emirate of Dubai, is the richest horse race in the world. Baffert won with Silver Charm (1998) and Captain Steve (2000).

Bob Baffert had two colts in the 1998 Kentucky Derby—favorite Indian Charlie and eventual winner Real Quiet.

GROWING UP

I GREW UP on a cattle ranch in Arizona. My father bought a few Quarter Horses. Quarter Horses run really short distances (350 to 400 yards). When I got old enough, my father decided to open a ranch. At age 14, I became his exercise boy. I was also the groom and basically performed every job you could think of on the farm. During my high school years I decided to try and be a jockey. I was little at the time so it worked. But I then had a growth spurt. I rode a few races, but I didn't really have the talent to be a jockey. I won 25 races and had a lot of fun with it. After I went to the University of Arizona, I figured I could either get a job or become a horse trainer. So, I became a horse trainer.

LEARNING TO TRAIN

I WAS A self-taught trainer. It took me forever to learn, but I finally learned my own way. I was always around good horsemen and that is the bottom line for having success. If you grow up with horsemen and you are around horses, you develop a keen sense of their personalities and what they are like. You can give me a wild horse and I can break him myself. I could work with him and do everything from scratch. Not a lot of trainers can do that.

I used to break all of my own horses. I would just get on them, work them, and teach them how to run. I don't get on them anymore. When you are developing young horses, horsemanship really counts. Some guys are better with older horses that are already seasoned runners. I am really good with young horses because of horsemanship. I know what I need to do with them and how much I can or can't lean on them. It's all experience that's based on trial and error. I know what we can do with a specific horse and try to learn from the mistakes I've made. When I purchase horses, I know what I can live with and what I can't.

I have always trained horses the same way. I like to get a horse really fit so they're in top shape before I run them. You can get your hands on a really good horse, but the tough part is keeping them healthy and sound. There are a lot of things involved. There are always one or two horses that get hurt. I probably have close to 100 horses. A lot of the horses (about 20 to 25) are at various farms being rested and healed-up.

OWNERS

I WORK WITH about 20 to 25 owners. It's important for me to feel comfortable with them. There are many good owners out there. However, there are also some good owners that go a little "wacko" when they get a really good horse. You never really know an owner until he gets a good horse. I've known some owners that will even get divorced over a horse. They can really go crazy. All of a sudden they show up one day and they decide that they are going to take over. It takes the fun out of it. I'll listen to a lot of their input, but when they get goofy on me, I'll just split ways with them. Once they get like that, you're going to split with them eventually anyway.

Owners and trainers must have mutual respect. My owners know I don't wake up in the morning thinking of ways to ruin their horse or get them beat. They know that I'm very competitive and I hate to lose.

TRAINING IS NONSTOP WORK

I WORK SEVEN days a week. Monday and Tuesday are very busy. It's very rare that I will take a vacation. You are in the hot seat constantly, so it's difficult to take time off. When you have high-profile horses and owners to deal with, you always have that feeling that things might go wrong. I actually went skiing for the first time this year. I haven't skied in 15 years. I went to get into my ski clothes and they didn't fit!

PRIVATE WORLD

NOBODY TALKS ABOUT his or her horses too much. We live in a very secretive world. We don't talk about our horses because we don't want people to get the wrong information. That's why you will sometimes hear a trainer saying his horse is not feeling well because of a bruised foot. The bruise on the foot is an easy way out. You can't tell the public what he really has if there's something there. Horses are like athletes. Every good athlete has something wrong with him, and they work through it. The public, however, has a tendency to overemphasize everything. Fortunately, there are those gifted animals that never get hurt regardless of what you do with them. Silver Charm was one of those gifted horses. I trained him so hard and he took every bit of it. He was so tough.

Trainer Bob Baffert

MY TEAM

I HAVE A pretty good team and we all work together. I have about 16 employees and four assistants. They work hard, but they do get time off. In fact, I make sure they get vacations. Otherwise, they would get burnt out. I don't get burnt out because I'm always looking for that big, "freaky" horse that nobody has ever seen before. Everybody wants a Secretariat in his or her life.

I usually get to the track about 7:00 a.m. I think that keeps me from burning out. Most trainers get to the barn around 4:30 or 5:00 a.m. My barn starts at 5:00 a.m. when my team takes out the horses that are going to walk that day. If I got here at 5:00 in the morning, I probably would have burnt out by now. I like to have a little life. Most trainers go to bed at 7:00 p.m., but I go to bed at 10:00. I get to the barn late, but once I get here, I stay most of the day.

TRIPLE CROWN

THE TRIPLE CROWN is really exciting. There is nothing like the Kentucky Derby. When you have a lot of really good horses, you get used to winning. When you know you are supposed to win and you do, it's a big deal. If you've been through it before you're used to it. But the Kentucky Derby is a whole different ball game. It's the only race that when you win it's truly the ultimate high.

The 2001 Preakness and Belmont Stakes winner, Point Given.

Baffert, who began his career conditioning Quarter Horses, has emerged as one of America's leading Thoroughbred trainers in a relatively short period of time.

FAVORITE HORSE

SILVER CHARM WAS my favorite Thoroughbred. He was the horse I won my first Derby with. He is such a neat horse. He really gave us a lot of fun. The people that owned him, Bob and Beverly Lewis, are the greatest owners in the world. They let you run everything and probably have had the best luck of any owner I've ever worked with.

HANDICAPPING

HORSE TRAINERS ARE the worst handicappers. You can't gamble and train horses. You can only be successful at one or the other. I rarely gamble. Once in a while I might see a horse whose odds I think should be lower and I'll bet a few bucks on him. One of the things

148

you'll see with trainers is that they'll start getting nervous and changing their mind the closer they get to the race. You start thinking of all the things that can go wrong. Three days out you'll say the horse can't lose. Two days out you'll say it has a really good chance. The day before the race you'll say it looks pretty tough. The day of the race, you'll say I don't know, it's going to be tough.

When you are a long shot, you don't worry about stuff like that. When you are not expected to win, everything is smooth. When you are expected to win, that's when it gets tough. A lot of people bet my horses because I put them in the right spots. I don't know why, but sometimes when you have two horses in a race the longest shot wins the race.

BREEDING

I ACTUALLY OWN a couple of mares. But I'm not really good at breeding. When I'm buying young horses, I do most of the buying for the owners. I kind of have to because buying a horse is a lot like a marriage. You are going to be with the horse for a long time and you have to make sure you're both compatible.

TRAINING 2-YEAR-OLDS VERSUS 3-YEAR-OLDS

TWO-YEAR-OLDS are younger, so you have to teach and show them everything—how to run, how to relax, when not to go, and stuff like that. You have to learn what their styles are and you can't rush them. Some horses want to go right to the front and they don't want to look back. They are very competitive animals. There are also some horses that don't like to be looked in the eye by another horse. They can't take that kind of pressure. When horses are out there by themselves they get a lot of courage and a big heart, which allows them to keep going. You have to know their personalities and what kind of track they like. There are a lot of grass horses out there because they don't like getting dirt kicked in their face. Horses that get dirt in their face for the first time will sometimes hop around like a kangaroo! Some get used to it, but others can't stand it. I like 2-year-olds because they are like little kids. You get to teach them and they can be future stars. You usually know by age 2 whether or not a horse is a Kentucky Derby contender.

JOCKEY SELECTION

I TRY TO pick a jockey that fits the race style. There are some jockeys that are better in one type of race scenario as opposed to another. Some riders excel on the lead and are capable of sneaking away from the pack. Other riders are good at the big-money races. These types of jockeys don't get too excited. They are still nervous, but they don't turn into mush.

Baffert and jockey Gary Stevens have teamed-up to win some of racings biggest events

ADVICE FOR OTHER TRAINERS

YOU HAVE TO be dedicated and really love the game to succeed as a trainer. It's like being a coach for a professional team in that you're totally consumed. It's 24/7. You really have to love the animals. There is some pressure, but it's well worth it. I've been in the business for 30 years and I still love every minute of it.

18

The Thrill of Thoroughbred Ownership

BEHIND THE SCENES WITH OWNER BARRY SCHWARTZ

arry Schwartz is one of the most prominent figures in Thoroughbred racing. He has dedicated his time, energy, and passion to the sport. In Schwartz's nonracing life, he is the co-founder as well as chairman and chief executive officer of Calvin Klein. Schwartz also

Barry Schwartz, chairman of the New York Racing Association (NYRA), has been involved with all aspects of horse racing. Over the years, his involvement in the sport has grown beyond race horse ownership and breeding.

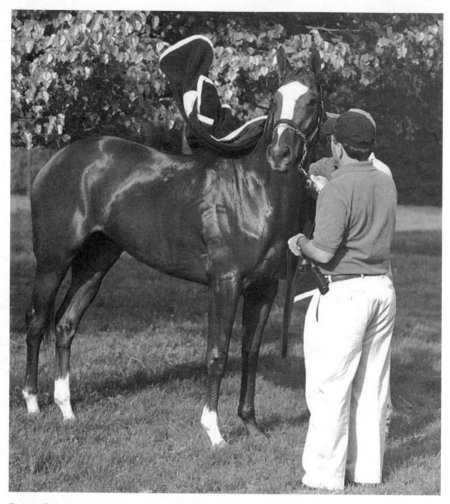

Barry Schwartz regularly keeps 50 to 60 horses on his farm.

breeds in New York at his own Stonewall Farms. He is a member of The Jockey Club, and has taken on the added challenge and responsibility of becoming chairman of the New York Racing Association (NYRA).

Schwartz gives us insight into the exciting world of Thoroughbred ownership. He not only discusses how he became involved in the sport, but also gives expert advice for those who are just starting out in the game and thinking about purchasing their first Thoroughbred.

FOR THE LOVE OF RACING

I CAME FROM a neighborhood where everyone gambled. They bet on sports and horses. A lot of older kids I hung around with went to the racetrack. So, I started going with them when I was about 15 years old. We always loved going. The racetrack was a very exciting place. When I was 19, I was traveling with a friend of mine and I passed through Lexington, Kentucky. I saw the gates at Calumet Farm and we just drove in. That was my first realization of what this whole sport was about—white fences, beautiful rolling fields, and horses grazing. We were enthralled with the whole thing.

THE HORSE RACING BUSINESS

I BOUGHT MY first horse in 1978. I was in business with a man who owned the company that was the licensee for our jeans (Calvin Klein) and he was a very successful owner. He had raced a champion filly named Chris Evert. Occasionally, I would go to the races with him. One day I told him that I would really like to get a horse. So, he introduced me to a trainer that was working for him. One thing led to another and I bought my first racehorse.

I've had as many as 220 horses at one time. It was only for a brief period, however, because the large amount really got out of hand. I also bought a farm and it turned out to be one of the greatest investments. I always enjoyed farms and wanted to have one. In 1979, I bought a piece of property in Westchester County, which is located in New York State. It is the largest piece of open land in the county, other than the Rockefeller estate. From a financial perspective, I have done very well in the horse business because the land is worth an enormous amount of money.

The most horses I've ever had on the farm was about 100, and even that is too big a number. Right now I have about 50 to 60. The farm is approximately 750 acres. I could probably keep five times as many horses if I wanted, but this is a manageable number. I am also building a house on the property, so I can live there at some point.

I do some breeding on the farm, but most of my mares are sent to Kentucky to be bred. When the breeding is complete, they come back to New York so I can register them. The stallions, however, are from Kentucky. I can breed from the best bloodlines in the world in Kentucky and still have horses that are New York-bred. There are financial incentives for raising registered New York-bred horses.

BREEDING TO RACE

UNLIKE MANY BREEDERS, I breed all my horses to race. I'll sell a few, but I'm mostly interested in getting them to the track. They're raised and broken on my farm before they're 2 years old. Then, they are sent to Florida for training and usually come back six months later. Most horses go into training in September and October of their yearling year. Hopefully, if all goes well, they can get to a racetrack by April of their 2-year-old year. I keep most of my horses in New York, but I do send a small string to California and a small group to Florida. I have trainers in each of those states that work with the horses.

FULL-TIME JOB

I DON'T REALLY think I'm a typical owner. I spend a lot of time with the horses because it's a very important part of my life and I have a large operation. A good deal of my time is spent overseeing my own horses and racing operations. Certain times of the year take up more time than others, such as when you are matching up your mares with prospective stallions and working on breeding.

SYNDICATION/PARTNERSHIPS OR INDIVIDUAL OWNERSHIP

I OWN MOST of the horses outright. I own a few horses with partners, but these are people that I'm very friendly with. It's usually a 50-50 partnership. As far as syndication goes, the only syndications I would be involved with would be stallions. Actually, anyone that buys a share in a stallion is part of a syndication. If you buy a share in a horse, you're usually partners with 40 or 50 other people. It's really not a partnership per se.

COMMUNICATION COUNTS

I SPEAK TO my New York trainer (main trainer) every morning. Basically, we discuss the aspects of all the horses in training. We'll discuss where and when to race each horse. The trainer will always ask for my opinion, but the final decision is usually his. He knows the horses better than anyone does. I don't know if all owners operate this way, but the intelligent ones do.

Deciding whether or not to enter a horse in one of the Triple Crown races is an easy decision. The horse tells you. I ran a horse in the 1990 Derby and two other times. With the exception of the filly I ran in 1999 (which was an extraordinary decision because it was a filly) the decision to run is easy to make. Normally, if you have a top-caliber 3-year-old and he has demonstrated he can do the mile-and-a-quarter distance, it's a no-brainer. You can usually tell if your horse belongs. If it can win one of the Derby prep races or at least come close, such as finishing 2nd or 3rd, then the horse has shown that it belongs.

It is very important to have good chemistry with your trainer. Many owners will change trainers periodically. It's a question of the level of communication they want to have and the chemistry between the two. If you're not a good match, you have to end it. If you spend a lot of time at the track you get to know the other trainers and you see what they do with the stock they get. Most trainers are public trainers and train for more than one person. If you have nice horses, however, it's unlikely that a trainer would turn you down.

ADVICE FOR POTENTIAL OWNERS

IF YOU ENJOY racing and you're interested in owning horses, there's probably nothing more gratifying. I love the sport. Horse ownership is the most exciting thing I've ever done in my life. There's no feeling like winning a race. My advice to the potential owner would be to really look at the game carefully and use that same carefulness when selecting your trainer. Think of it as your own business. When I first started in the business, I thought I really understood racing. But knowing how to read the *Daily Racing Form* does not mean you understand the business. I made many mistakes the first five years, which probably could have been avoided if I had somebody that really understood what was going on and had given me good advice.

The great thing about racing is that it's not as tough as you'd think to compete against the large operations. It's not like the richest guy is going to buy the best horses and win all the races. Jim Hill and Mickey Taylor proved that when they paid $17,500 for Seattle Slew, who became the greatest horse of the decade. It is a level playing field and everyone has a chance.

OWNER'S BOX

AS AN OWNER it's really nice to be able to watch the race from anywhere at the track. It's fun to watch from the owner's box, but it's also nice to wear jeans, eat hot dogs, and lie in the grass between races like the general crowd does day in and day out.

NEW YORK RACING ASSOCIATION RESPONSIBILITIES

AS CHAIRMAN, I have the responsibility of running three racetracks—Aqueduct, Belmont, and Saratoga. Essentially, my role is to teach, plan, and make decisions regarding the direction we want to go in. Basically, I'm trying everything I can to make the racetracks better.

THE NAME GAME

As an owner you get to name your horses. But it's not always that easy. I start by asking everyone I know for opinions. I get many suggestions from the people that work at Calvin Klein. It's quite common for owners to name their horses after famous people. But this can create problems. First, you have to get the person's permission. Then, if the horse doesn't perform well, you'd be surprised how insulted some people become. I few years back I named a horse after David Geffen. I only wanted to use the first same, so I registered "David." Fortunately, the name hadn't been used before. David made me very proud and he was a very good horse. I didn't ask Geffen for permission, since I had only used his first name. Anyway, everyone I knew said that I named the horse after Geffen. And since he was such a good horse, I agreed with their assumption!

And, just for the record, I would never name a horse Calvin Klein. That would be too tacky!

Fun Fact

Naming racehorses may seem like fun, but it's not as easy as you would think. The Jockey Club has to approve all names and ensures that inappropriate names are not used. Most owners use some tie-in to the pedigree of the horse. Clever examples include Blond in a Motel, by Bates Motel, and Prenup, by Smarten out of Homewrecker.

Watching and Enjoying Races

A Day at the Races

A DAY AT THE races for a typical fan can start early in the morning or even the night before. Some racing fans will study the *Daily Racing Form* the night before they attend the track and map out their race selections beforehand. If you're a morning person, some racetracks offer a special breakfast program where fans have the opportunity to visit the track for a behind-the-scenes tour of the facility. This is not only a great way to spend a warm spring or summer morning, but also a great chance to watch some of the horses' morning workouts.

One of the first things you should do upon your arrival at the track is purchase a copy of *Daily Racing Form*. The *Form* has most of the information required to place your bets. You'll see information on horses, jockeys, trainers, distance, types of races, post positions, betting numbers, past-performance data, and morning-line betting odds (see Chapter 12). Don't be intimidated by the amount of information provided. Instead, have some fun studying and make it a learning experience. You may even want to make notes in the

It's not uncommon to have a group of racing fans congregating at the track's finish line in order to get the best view.

margin as to what handicapping factors are important to you and compare these notes with friends. Make a game out of it!

Taking a trip to the paddock area to watch the horses get saddled is always exciting. This gives you the first opportunity to inspect the physical characteristics of each horse. You'll be able to see them without their jockeys on board, which is not the case in the post parade. After the jockeys mount up, the horses head for the track. When you hear the familiar sound of the bugler, you'll know it is time for the post parade. Take a minute or two and examine the horses during this procession. The post parade occurs approximately 10 minutes prior to post time. Make some notes in your program as to which horses look physically fit and eager to run.

HELPFUL HINT

There are many different areas where you can watch the races: your seat or box in the clubhouse or grandstand, the track "apron" (the open area in front of the stands) and especially on the in-house TV's, which are placed all around the track so you never miss a minute!

162

IT'S POST TIME!

AFTER PLACING YOUR bets, go scope out an area to watch the race. There's no right or wrong location to watch a race. It's basically what works best for you. For a great close-up view of these magnificent athletes, you might want to find a spot directly along the track's rail. If you're interested in seeing the larger panorama of the race, grab a spot in the grandstand or clubhouse seating area. Pack a pair of binoculars and you'll be able to follow the running of the race even more closely. If you don't want to watch the race live, there are dozens of TV's located inside the track that show the running of the race. It doesn't really matter where you watch, just as long as you and your friends are comfortable.

Fun Fact

As with most other sporting events, a pair of binoculars provides an up-close view of all the racing action. You can examine the horse's body language during the post parade and watch him run all the way from the starting gate to the finish line.

The track announcer signals that the race is about to begin by saying, "It is now post time." Once the horses break from the gate, feel free to yell or hold your breath (just don't pass out!). While at the track, you're sure to witness all types of interesting ways that racing fans root for their favorite horses. For example, you might see a person impersonating a jockey by hitting his newspaper against the side of his leg, or doing something that looks like a double-handed fist pound. There's also the popular jump-up-and-down-and-hop-on-one-foot move! Basically, anything goes.

Once the race is over (and the results have been declared official), you can go back to any of the betting windows (not just the one where you placed your bet) and collect your winnings. You can cash your ticket at any time during the day (just be sure not to acciden-tally throw it away). You don't need to collect your winnings imme-diately after the race. Technically, you have an entire year to cash your winning ticket. But odds are you won't want to wait that long! After a race is declared official, you have another 25 minutes or so before the start of the next race. You can use that time to celebrate your victory, study the next race, drown your sorrows, eat, or just hang out. Tracks normally have between eight and 10 races a day.

CITATION

Many tracks such as a Hialiah, feature statues of famous racehorses.

PLANNING AHEAD

THE MOST IMPORTANT thing to remember at the track is to have fun. In order to do so, be sure not to overextend yourself and leave the track penniless. Remember this popular racetrack slogan: "Bet with your head, not over it." A good strategy is to allocate your betting money beforehand so you'll know exactly how much you can afford to lose (consider it your entertainment for the day). Also be sure to set aside some money for food and drinks. Most tracks (unlike many

A Day at the Races

sporting facilities) allow you to bring your own food and beverages. But if you haven't planned ahead or just want to take in the real flavor of the day, make sure you have enough money to sample some of the traditional track fare.

Even if you're not into wagering, there are plenty of things to keep you entertained at the track. Some people spend all day watching the beautiful horses and soaking up the social scene. One of the thrills of visiting the track is watching all the action that takes place before and after each race. The grooms prepare the horses, the jockeys get last-minute instructions from the trainers, and the serious handicappers busily jot notes into their programs or *Daily Racing Forms*. One of the fun things about the track is watching the other fans. What makes racing so exciting is that every person has his or her own unique experience at the track.

INTERVIEW WITH JAY PRIVMAN

One horse-racing fan who knows how to spend a day at the races is Jay Privman of Daily Racing Form. *Privman is the national correspondent for the paper and is responsible for covering horse racing's biggest national news events. He provides exclusive coverage of the Triple Crown and Breeders' Cup races, and also tracks many of the prep races leading up to these events. Privman is no stranger to the racetrack. His first experience with horse racing began when he attended the races with his family. He was only 11 at the time. In 1982 Privman attended his first Kentucky Derby. Twenty years later, he has become a permanent fixture at the prestigious event.*

Privman provides some funny and interesting insight into the sport and describes some of the things a fan might expect to see while attending a day at the races.

BB: *How did you get into racing?*
JP: In the late 1960's, a local TV show used to show the feature race

on Saturday afternoons. I watched all the time and loved the competition. I liked the fact that horse racing was held outdoors. I admired the beautiful horses and the mental handicapping part of the game. Looking back, it's hard to believe that I was that interested in racing at such an early age. I would make my own picks out of the paper.

When I was 12 years old, I was going to Santa Anita and Hollywood Park once a month. My parents would make bets for me. At age 20, in my junior year of college, I started working part-time at the Los Angeles *Daily News* as a sports journalist. The paper didn't have a horse-racing writer and they really wanted to expand their coverage. They decided to allow me to cover the big races. The first day in the paper, I picked six winners on top. The next day I picked two on top. When I graduated, they made me full-time.

BB: *Since you have worked many years in the industry, what have been some of the greatest races and rivalries you've experienced?*

JP: The greatest rivalry and probably some of the best races occurred between Easy Goer and Sunday Silence during their 1989 Triple Crown. The Preakness Stakes was the most exciting of the three races when an unbelievable stretch duel developed between the two horses. In a fantastic run for the wire, Sunday Silence edged Easy Goer by a nose. Then, later in the year, both horses ran in the Breeders' Cup Classic when Horse of the Year honors were on the line. Sunday Silence beat him again. They ran against each other four times that year and Sunday Silence won three of those intense battles.

BB: *Any other special horses that stand out like this pair?*

JP: One favorite horse of mine was a mare named Flawlessly. About 10 years ago in the early 1990's, she was the champion female turf runner. I liked her because she had this really big white blaze down her face and she was a distinctive-looking horse. Flawlessly was a top-class turf runner and won the Ramona Handicap (one of Del Mar's biggest races for her division) for three straight years.

BB: *Do you remember any races where something crazy happened?*

JP: The craziest thing I've ever witnessed occurred two years ago at the Preakness Stakes in Baltimore. Earlier in the day, which was the fifth or sixth race on the card, an inebriated fan ran on the track during the race! It was very scary. The horses managed to avoid him, but my heart was in my throat. I can't believe the guy didn't get run over.

BB: *What types of horse-racing superstitions have you witnessed or been part of?*

JP: I do know of a couple of real funny stories. The winningest jockey of all time (Laffit Pincay Jr.) wears his underwear inside out every day when he rides! There is also another guy, Gary Garber, who owns a horse named Flame Thrower. Gary wore this loud Hawaiian shirt the first time this horse ran and won. So, he kept on wearing the shirt for each start thereafter. Flame Thrower finally got beat in his fifth race, so Gary got rid of the Hawaiian shirt and started wearing something else. I've also seen trainers wear the same clothes after their horses win. Handicappers have a lot of rituals. I used to do really weird stuff. I had these borderline obsessive behaviors when I was handicapping that I have fortunately been able to grow out of.

BB: *What were some of them?*

JP: I used to tap my finger when I was reading at my desk. I would have to do it four times because I wore number 4 when I was in Little League. I know it makes absolutely no sense, but I would do stuff like that.

BB: *What changes have you seen in the racing industry and what further alterations would you like to see take place?*

JP: Well, the biggest change has been the number of people who actually come to live races. When I first got into the sport, there was no off-track betting. If you wanted to legally bet on the horses, you had to come to the racetrack. That's no longer necessary, so the crowds are smaller. I wish the on-track attendance would increase, but I'm doubtful that will happen with all the simulcasting and off-track venues.

I also think there is entirely too much racing on a day-to-day basis. And I am really not crazy about the medication rules. The one thing I would like to say (I guess this is a benign comment) is that I think jockeys are tremendously gifted and courageous athletes. Having worked with them and covered them, I think that most of them are good guys. I really wish there were more of an appreciation for jockeys on several levels—not from just a fan standpoint, but also from an endorsement standpoint. I would like to see jockeys appear on TV more often. Several years ago there was a California jockey named Fernando Toro who has since retired. Fernando's specialty was riding grass races. His nickname was "Toro on the turf." I always thought it would have been a great ad for Toro lawn mowers to put Fernando on one and have him drive down the turf course at Hollywood. I would like to see jockeys in more commercial settings where the public would see them more often. I think they deserve it.

BB: *Do you have any final thoughts for our new racing fans who are attending the track for the first time?*

JP: I think the track is kind of like wine appreciation. The more you know about it, the better you'll like it. But you are not going to like it if you drink eight different glasses of wine the first time you go to a wine tasting. You have to go and enjoy the atmosphere of the track. To me, the gambling at the track is fun and enjoyable. But it shouldn't be the only reason why you go there. I think there is a real appreciation for the horse and jockey that you can get. One of the best things you can do is go to the paddock before the races and just look at the horses. You can really get close to the participants and that's one thing that I think is really neat about the sport.

20

How to Throw a Great Kentucky Derby Party

TIPS FROM PARTY-GIVER EXTRAORDINAIRE
PATRICIA BARNSTABLE BROWN

Patricia Barnstable Brown has been a fan of Thoroughbred racing her entire life. She was born in Louisville, Kentucky, and going to Churchill Downs and the Kentucky Derby was an integral part of her life, as well as that of her twin sister. Despite her successful career as a Ford model (Patricia and her sister were featured in the Double Mint twins campaign), she still managed to make it home every year for the Kentucky Derby. The Derby became a source of pride and enjoyment for her family. After getting married *and having a son, she decided to become involved in charity work. Patricia dedicates her time to fund-raising for research to cure diabetes, which her husband was diagnosed with in 1991. In 1989, before her husband was diagnosed with the disease, she put together what she thought would be a small Derby party to raise money for diabetes research.*

With close to 500 people at the first party, including a number of celebrities such as Patrick Duffy, Lloyd Bridges, Dixie Carter, and Hal

Holbrook, her first Kentucky Derby party was a big success. Brown's party has become legendary since the inaugural event. Each year, she raises substantial sums of money for the Diabetes Foundation (at least a quarter of a million dollars a year, which is matched by the state). The party attracts celebrities and fans from all across the nation to witness the innovative themes, Southern hospitality, and the fun and excitement of Derby fever.

Patricia Barnstable Brown explains the details involved in planning such a grand event and gives some advice for planning your own scaled-down party at home. She also offers some tips for what to wear if you find yourself lucky enough to attend the Kentucky Derby.

DECIDING ON A THEME

WE HAVE A different theme each year because that seems to be expected and anticipated. I usually choose the theme the summer before Derby Day. For some reason, I don't feel settled until I know what it's going to be. It takes time and it can be difficult to agree on a particular theme. One year we changed the theme four times. We had many suggestions, but nothing stuck. It keeps getting harder and harder to come up with new themes. And, as of yet, I haven't had to recycle any of them.

PAST THEMES

ONE THEME WE did was Egypt. I had a 40-foot pyramid in the front yard. It was completely done with wood and gold cloth. I have this long winding driveway that was painted blue for the Nile River. I even had camels brought in from Indianapolis. I also did "The Wizard of Oz" one year. I had a hot-air balloon and eight-foot poppies everywhere. I also brought in munchkins and, of course, beautiful ruby slippers.

Another theme was New York. I had six stages in my front yard and each one had a different Broadway play performing on them.

My favorite theme was probably "Babes in Toyland." I had a bunch of children dressed up as toys. I had a 100-plus-foot jack-in-the-box hot-air balloon. Everything was toys. Then, I had a light display of a train, toys, and jack-in-the-box. This year's theme (2001) was "Cinderella." We had a whole fairy tale acted out on six different stages. We had carriages drawn by miniature horses, a Cinderella light display, the castle, the glass slippers, and a lot of white, twinkly lights. It was a huge extravaganza.

FROM THEME TO REALITY

AFTER WE DECIDE on a theme, we get a local dance group involved. They usually start preparing about six weeks before the party. They love it and are very excited to help out. They build the stages, get the costumes, and arrange the performances. They have decorators, who help get different props on loan.

FOOD

WE DON'T COORDINATE the food with the different themes. We stick to strictly Kentucky-style food such as fresh asparagus, corn pudding, beef tenderloin, country ham on biscuits, and fresh strawberries dipped in chocolate. As for drinks, we serve mint juleps (of course), champagne, and a full bar.

ATTIRE

THE ATTIRE FOR the evening is strictly black tie. The men come in tuxes and the women break out their extravagant ball gowns.

CELEBRITY GUEST LIST

OVER THE YEARS, I have gathered a group of loyal friends that I can always count on to come to the party. They mark it on their calendars. This year our honorary chairperson was George Strait and he always gets up and performs. Dixie Carter and Bo Derek come every year as well. We always get new and exciting celebrities that are fresh on the scene as well. In past years, we've had the Backstreet Boys and Kid Rock. This year, some of the celebrities included Peyton Manning, Anne Heche, Warren Moon, and Michael Imperioli ("The Sopranos").

ENTERTAINMENT

THE ENTERTAINMENT IS not tied to the theme of the party and we always seem to get great bands to play. Last year, it was so spectacular. We had John Michael Montgomery, Travis Tritt, George Strait, Chris Isaac, Chaka Kahn, and the Backstreet Boys. It was amazing. This year we had Kid Rock, Mary Wilson from the Supremes, Joe Diffie, and Meat Loaf. We even had Bo Derek, Roseanne, Pamela Sue Anderson, and Carol Alt get up on stage.

DERBY DAY

THE DAY AFTER the party I'm very exhausted. But I quickly energize myself because it's the Derby and I'm responsible for hosting all the celebrities that come to the party the night before.

ADVICE FOR OTHER PARTY GIVERS

IF YOU'RE THINKING of having your own Kentucky Derby party, it's important to have everything planned out well in advance. Most importantly, remember to enjoy yourself. If you have a party that includes watching the Derby live, I would do some type of betting pool. This way, when people watch the race, they have an active participation in who wins and a reason to cheer for a particular horse. As for decorations, I would choose a horse-type theme, which could involve little jockey silks, mint-julep glasses and drinks, and little horses strategically placed around the party. Mint-julep drinks are important to have on Derby Day. Whether you like them or not, they are very unusual and definitely a conversation piece. The Southern hospitality, elegance, and fashion are all so important to Derby Day.

FASHION FOR DERBY DAY

PEOPLE ALWAYS WANT to make sure they have the right thing on come Derby Day. The style of the Derby is world renowned. Fashion is a big part of it—the big hats, suits, etc. Many of the big parties the night before have women wearing long gowns and jewels. If you don't have all of that, I think the Derby would be missing something. No other sport has that extravagance the night before or even just the ambiance that day. Everybody calls me with his or her fashion questions for Derby Day. You'd be surprised how much time and effort people put into it. They get custom-made hats to match their suits and shop for just the right outfits. The ladies all wear hats and spring suits or dresses. It seems like the hats go best with suits. The men wear sports coats. Ties are optional for the men but sometimes they wear hats as well. Derby Day is the time to bring out your bright colors and pastels.

As for shoes, comfort sometimes goes out the door. There can be a lot of walking around, but you'd be surprised at the number of women (me included) who wear high heels. For many people, pain doesn't seem to be an issue, even if you are unable to walk for the next week! It's just part of Derby Weekend. It's a real social weekend and that's what makes it so much fun. It's the place to be and to be seen.

Racing Strategy

The Racing Secretary

INTERVIEW WITH RACING SECRETARY MIKE LAKOW

*T*he racing secretary has one of the most important and difficult jobs at the track. The racing secretary and his staff work tirelessly to put on races that are competitive and of interest to the betting public. Although this may not seem that difficult, when you consider the length of the racing season (practically all year) and the vast number of horses, it is easy to see that this is a demanding position.

Mike Lakow, racing secretary for the New York Racing Association (NYRA), has the pressure-filled job of writing the condition book, assigning stall space, and filling each race in the New York area. Lakow explains his day-to-day activities and passion for the sport.

BB: *How did you first become involved in horse racing?*
ML: I've always had a great love for Thoroughbred racing. I can recall going to school when I was 9 or 10 years old and sneaking a *Daily Racing Form* under all my books. I was never into gam-

bling, but I just loved horses and the sport itself. One summer I had the opportunity to work at the Atlantic City racetrack in the racing office. Once you have a love for something, it's hard to escape it (not that I wanted to). I just kept working hard and finally I got to where I am today.

BB: *How long have you been in your current position?*
ML: Five years.

BB: *What do you do and what type of responsibilities do you have?*
ML: First, I have to do a lot of work with delegating stalls. The reason I'm bringing that up now is because I have about three or four thousand horses with stall applications for the winter meet. We try to bring in the best horses and horsemen to fill the card. We want to have the best racing in the world in New York. My office works very hard at achieving that goal. We have to gather all the stall applications, categorize every horse, and then break up the horses so we have comparative racing. The goal is to give everyone a chance to win. In addition, every two to three weeks, I write the condition book.

BB: *Is it considered more prestigious if a trainer has stalls at one of the NYRA tracks, or is it just more convenient to be stabled there?*
ML: The Belmont spring meet and the Saratoga meet are extremely popular and there's a real need for stall space. The winter meets are not as prestigious, but that's no reason to downplay them. It's a long campaign to have to run your better horses in December and January and keep them going for the entire racing cycle.

BB: *How many stalls, for example, would you allot for Saratoga?*
ML: There are about 1,600 stalls at Saratoga and 1,900 stalls at Belmont. You can have stalls at Belmont for the Saratoga meet [and then van the horses upstate to race].

BB: *How many horses apply?*
ML: We have about 4,000 horses apply at Saratoga. It's difficult allotting stalls, but it goes along with the job. It's a heartache for

people to have to find another place to go, especially if they have families or live in New York.

BB: *What kinds of decisions go into allotting the stalls?*

ML: We look for trainers that have the background or reputation of being knowledgeable with quality horses. I have to limit the stalls per trainer. The maximum in New York is 44. And if they have 44 stalls, they probably have around 60 to 70 horses. A lot of trainers, if they apply for 10 horses, don't necessarily have 10 horses ready to run at that time.

BB: *Does anyone have the 44-stall maximum?*

ML: Yes, there are probably around 10 trainers who have the maximum.

BB: *What happens if they don't use all the stalls they have been allotted, or if they have more horses than they have stalls for?*

ML: If they don't have space for all their horses, I can't help them. If they don't fill up their stalls, the stalls will revert back to the association [NYRA]. Before reverting them back, I'll talk to the trainers and find out what's going on. I try to accommodate them as much as possible.

BB: *Is it difficult to get enough horses to come to the winter meets?*

ML: Right now it's not, but it was a problem in the past. The purses are high in New York and if the trainers' horses have the right credentials, the horsemen want to be here.

BB: *What goes into writing the condition book?*

ML: Every horse and race category is entered into the book. We have nine to 11 races in it each day, which includes the race type and names of the horses running. The book comes out a week or two in advance so the trainers can plan accordingly. Our goal is to make every horse a winner, so it's important to mix the races up the best you can. For the sake of the fans, I also try to mix up the race distances.

BB: *Is it difficult to come up with enough good horses to fill each race?*

ML: Absolutely. Sometimes I get lucky and other times I make mistakes. As of right now, I'm pleased with how things are going.

BB: *Do you have any advice for the novice handicapper? What would you say, for example, is a good angle for handicappers to look at in a maiden race?*

ML: Well, I've never been a gambler. Some people are very good at it. In this case I would certainly look at the trainer and see how he is doing at the current meet. Trainers go in cycles and right now we have a few trainers doing really well.

BB: *How do you factor in the weight requirements?*

ML: In New York, most of our stakes races ($75,000 up to $1 million) are handicaps. I gather the information from all the horses nominated to race (nominations are made two weeks prior to the particular stakes race). I try to formulate who is the best horse. Once that's decided, I try to figure out how much weight they should be given compared to the other horses in the same race. I try not to go with too big of a weight spread. I still like the best horse to win, but I want it to be competitive.

BB: *Is the trainer ever unhappy with the weight assignment the horse has been given?*

ML: Yes.

BB: *Do you ever try to alter the weight assignment to accommodate the trainer?*

ML: No. It's their prerogative not to run. And it does happen occasionally.

BB: *How do the stakes nominations work?*

ML: Two weeks before the scheduled stakes race, we have nominations. If you have a horse you want to run in a particular race, you call the office and ask to have it nominated for that race. Then, there's a fee you pay. If you have money in the bookkeeper's office, we'll take it out and apply it to the race.

BB: *Is it the same fee for every race?*

ML: No. I think it is one-tenth of 1 percent, or less. Some stakes are free. We have invitational races, like the Turf Classic, where there are no fees. We do this a couple times a year so we can have the best horses run with us and not have to pay.

Fun Fact

Trainers sometimes refuse to accept the weight assignments on their horses. In one instance, the great horse Spectacular Bid was assigned 136 pounds for the prestigious Marlboro Cup, while his rival Winter's Tale was given 13 pounds less. Unhappy with this state of affairs, Spectacular Bid's trainer, Bud Delp, took him out of the race.

BB: *What is the minimum number of horses you would schedule in a race?*

ML: A field of four is usually the smallest number we would schedule. In most cases, a four-horse field would probably be an allowance race. The owners and trainers that have horses in these types of races are usually prepping for stakes-race competition. In stakes races, I would say that a field of three would be the smallest we'd put together since the owners are paying to nominate and run.

BB: *What is the most number of horses you could race?*

ML: In our stakes-race programs, we usually go eight, nine, or 10 horses deep. The Kentucky Derby can run with 20.

BB: *After a day of racing, do you reassess what happened and how competitive the races were?*

ML: We certainly do that. Sometimes I shake my head and think what a terrible race that was, but most of the time things seem to run very smoothly.

One Mile

The
Homestretch

The Road to
the Triple Crown

TRIPLE FEAT

HORSE RACING IS a year-round sport, but many people don't start to focus their attention on horses until the "Run for the Roses"—the Kentucky Derby, which takes place on the first Saturday in May. The Kentucky Derby is the first and most prestigious leg of the Triple Crown series. Even people who know nothing about horse racing tune in to watch the Kentucky Derby. Winning the Triple Crown is undoubtedly the most strenuous feat in American Thoroughbred racing. A horse must win the Kentucky Derby at Churchill Downs, the Preakness Stakes at Pimlico, and the Belmont Stakes at Belmont Park in succession.

The Triple Crown races are run during a span of only five weeks from May to June at three different distances (1 ¼ miles, 1 ³⁄₁₆ miles, and 1 ½ miles). All three Triple Crown events have been run since the late 1800's, but the Kentucky Derby is the oldest continuously held sporting event in the United States. Only 3-year-olds can

1¼ MILES

▲ START ▲ FINISH

The Kentucky Derby, which is held annually at Churchill Downs, is the oldest continuously held sporting event in the United States. For the 3-year-olds competing in the race, it's their first test at the grueling 1-1/4-miles distance.

compete in the Triple Crown, so if a horse loses or misses a race, there is no opportunity to try again. In the history of Thoroughbred racing, only 11 horses have won all three events. The nation's best 3-year-olds are given the ultimate test of speed, stamina, and conditioning during their Triple Crown run. Winning even one of these races is considered impressive, but winning all three is legendary. There are a number of prep races leading up to the Triple Crown series. In the months of March and April, in particular, these attract national media coverage, and as the Derby draws closer everyone seems to have an opinion about the horses with the best prospects of competing at this level. The run for the Triple Crown is one of the most exciting times of the year in horse racing.

The Kentucky Derby is one of the world's most famous sporting events and is held at one of the country's most historic venues. The Derby takes place at Churchill Downs in Louisville, Kentucky, and attracts fans from all over the world. The race is 1 ¼ miles and has a purse of $1 million. Col. M. Lewis Clark built Churchill Downs with the intention of having a race that was similar to England's Epsom Derby. The first Kentucky Derby was run on May 17, 1875.

Fun Fact

In 1875, while carrying only 100 pounds, Aristides won the first Kentucky Derby. Aristides earned $2,850 for his winning effort.

In 1919, Sir Barton was the first Triple Crown winner.

Gallant Fox was the first horse ever to earn more than $300,000 in a single season.

Triple Crown winner, Omaha, who was the son of Gallant Fox, was the first and only Triple Crown winner to be sired by a Triple Crown winner.

1948 Triple Crown winner Citation was considered to be one of the greatest Thoroughbreds of all time.

The competitive rivalry between Alydar and Triple Crown winner Affirmed was one of the greatest of all time

The mighty Secretariat's Kentucky Derby track record still stands today.

Seattle Slew was the first horse to emerge undefeated from the Triple Crown.

Trainers take different paths to get their top 3-year-olds to the "big dance" on Derby Day. There are many preparatory races leading up to the Kentucky Derby, and these races attract the most promising Derby prospects. Some of the most notable prep races, which take place across the country on different weekends throughout the spring, include the Arkansas Derby, Blue Grass Stakes, Florida Derby, Louisiana Derby, Santa Anita Derby, and Wood Memorial. The 3-year-olds that run well in these select races usually perform reasonably well on Derby Day. Most of the Derby entrants are colts, but every so often a talented filly will compete against the boys. Any time a filly runs against the colts, there is a tremendous amount of attention and media coverage surrounding her. Among the many popular traditions associated with the Kentucky Derby are the parade of unique and colorful hats and the famous mint julep. According to Churchill Downs, over 80,000 mint juleps are served over Derby Weekend. If you are planning a Derby party, or you think you might be interested in creating this

MINT JULEP

2 cups sugar

2 cups water

Sprigs of fresh mint

Crushed ice

Kentucky bourbon

Silver julep cups

Make simple syrup by boiling sugar and water together for five minutes. Cool and place in a covered container with six or eight sprigs of fresh mint, then refrigerate overnight. Make one julep at a time by filling a julep cup with crushed ice, adding one tablespoon mint syrup and two ounces of Kentucky bourbon. Stir rapidly with a spoon to frost the outside of the cup. Garnish with a sprig of fresh mint.

unusual drink at home, the following recipe comes from Woodford
Reserve Bourbon.

Fun Fact

The first filly to win the Kentucky Derby was Regret in 1915
for owner Harry Payne Whitney. Since that time, only two
other fillies have managed victories in the race—Genuine
Risk (1980) and Winning Colors (1988).

THE PREAKNESS

The Preakness Stakes is the shortest of the three Triple Crown distances at 1 3/16 miles.

THE PREAKNESS IS held two weeks after the Kentucky Derby at
Pimlico Racetrack in Baltimore, Maryland. The Preakness Stakes is
the Mid-Atlantic region's largest sporting event, and over 100,000
racing fans crowd the stands and infield on the third weekend in
May. The race is 1 $\frac{3}{16}$ miles long. The Preakness Stakes began in
1873 and was named after a colt called Preakness, who won the
Dinner Party Stakes in 1870. The name is derived from Native
American culture. Racing fans often refer to the Preakness as the
middle jewel of the Triple Crown.

190

A horse named Survivor won the first Preakness Stakes by 10 lengths. Survivor was owned by John Chamberlain and won a purse of $2,050. Survivor's margin of victory continues to be the largest to date.

THE BLACK-EYED SUSAN

1 ¼ cup vodka
1 ¼ cup light rum
¾ cup triple sec
1 tbsp fresh lime juice
4 cups pineapple juice
4 cups orange juice
Ice ring with fruits
(pineapple, lemon, grapes)

Mixing instructions: Chill all ingredients. Just before serving combine in a punch bowl. Unmold ice ring and float in bowl. Serve in tall glasses. Makes 10 large servings.

One of the traditions at the Preakness is the "painting of the colors." A painter applies the colors of the victorious owner's silks to the weather vane at the top of the infield structure. Another tradition is the musical rendition of "Maryland My Maryland," which began when a bugler, moved by the spirit of the day, began playing Maryland's historic state song. The rest of the band, inspired by the music, joined in, and the crowd reacted enthusiastically. Just as the Derby has the mint julep as its official drink, the Preakness has the Black-Eyed Susan. Those who were ambitious enough to attempt to make the mint julep might find the Black-Eyed Susan a little easier to create.

BELMONT STAKES

THE BELMONT STAKES is the third jewel in racing's Triple Crown. The mile-and-one-half main track at Belmont Park is the largest in the country, and it is at that distance that the Belmont Stakes is contested. The Belmont Stakes is the oldest of the Triple Crown events

(1867), predating the Preakness by six years and the Kentucky Derby by eight. The winner of the first Kentucky Derby, Aristides, ran second in the Belmont of 1875. The first running of the Belmont Stakes took place at Jerome Park. The Belmont has halted 15 potential Triple Crown winners after their triumphs in the Derby and the Preakness. It is run in June at Belmont Park, which is located in Elmont, New York, about a half-hour's drive from New York City. In 1997, the track changed the anthem for its most famous race from "The Sidewalks of New York" to "New York, New York," which is played during the post parade.

START ▲ FINISH

The Belmont Stake's marathon distance tests each horse's stamina. A horse's pedigree plays a large part in determining whether it can handle the challenging distance.

Fun Fact

Ruthless, a filly owned by Francis Morris, won the first Belmont Stakes in 1867.

A new Belmont tradition is to paint the winning horse's colors on a four-foot iron jockey. If the winning horse is also a Triple Crown winner, the iron jockey will be moved to a special Triple Crown ring. The designated beverage of the Belmont is called the Belmont Breeze. It was created by Dale DeGroff, the head bartender at Manhattan's Rainbow Room and Windows on the World restaurants. The drink is based on a recipe for whiskey punch.

BREEDERS' CUP WORLD THOROUGHBRED CHAMPIONSHIP

ONCE THE TRIPLE Crown season is over, there are plenty of great races from around the country to keep racing enthusiasts occupied throughout the year. From Saratoga Springs, New York, to Del Mar, California, and everywhere in between, some of the best horses strut their stuff each weekend in various stakes events. The racing season really starts to intensify throughout the summer and fall and eventually leads up to the Breeders' Cup, World Thoroughbred Championship where the "best of the best" converge to wrap up the racing season. The Breeders' Cup is considered the Super Bowl of horse racing.

The annual event began in 1984 and is held in late October or early November. The Breeders' Cup hosts some of the best horses from around the world. Although the location changes from year to year, semi-regular sites include Churchill Downs, Belmont Park, Gulfstream Park, Hollywood Park, and Santa Anita. While the Triple Crown races are open only to the country's best 3-year-olds, the Breeders' Cup offers events for every age group and division. With the addition of the Filly and Mare Turf, which was run for the first time in 1999, the Breeders' Cup now consists of eight races with purses and awards totaling $13 million.

The races are run at different distances and over different racing surfaces. Horse racing's biggest day consists of the following line-up: $1 million Breeders' Cup Sprint, for 3-year-olds and up at six furlongs. $1 million Breeders' Cup Juvenile Fillies, for 2-year-old fillies at $1\frac{1}{16}$ miles. $2 million Breeders' Cup Distaff, for fillies and mares, 3-year-olds and up, at $1\frac{1}{8}$ miles. $1 million Breeders' Cup Mile, for 3-year-olds and up at one mile on the turf. $1 million Breeders' Cup Juvenile, for 2-year-olds at $1\frac{1}{16}$ miles. $1 million Bessener Trust Breeders' Cup Filly and Mare Turf, for fillies and mares, 3-year-olds and up, at $1\frac{3}{8}$ miles on the turf. $2 million Breeders' Cup Turf, for 3-year-olds and up, at $1\frac{1}{2}$ miles on the turf. $4 Million Breeders' Cup Classic, for 3-year-olds and up at $1\frac{1}{4}$ miles. The eight Breeders' Cup races are often the determining factor as to whether a horse will win a divisional championship or Horse of the Year honors.

This statue is the symbol of the Breeders' Cup.

The Immortals:
Racing's Legendary Champions

I N EVERY SPORT, fans have their favorite players and memories. Thoroughbred racing is no exception. Fans have their favorite horses and favorite racing moments. Choosing an overall favorite is simply a matter of personal preference. A person might like a particular horse because it won a number of races, or simply because he admires the horse's appearance or personality. In compiling any list of immortals, however, there are a few champions that stand out. This is not meant to be the definitive list of all racehorse legends, but simply a cross-section of some memorable Thoroughbreds to get you started. The list will help you become familiar with some of the names that you will hear in racing lore.

Man o' War (Foaled 1917)

MAN O' WAR compiled an amazing lifetime record of 20 wins and one second from 21 starts and accumulated nearly $250,000 in lifetime earnings. He set five American records at several different distances. Man o' War probably could have won more races and set even more records, but his owner, Samuel D. Riddle, retired him after his 3-year-old season because of the amount of weight he would have had to carry in his races as a 4-year-old. In his next-to-last start he carried 138 pounds. Despite the high weight assignments, Man o' War still managed to beat his opponents quite comfortably. After he was retired to stud, Man o' War also became a success in the breeding shed. His offspring included War Admiral, winner of the 1937 Triple Crown. When Man o' War died in 1947, he became the first horse to be embalmed and buried in a casket lined with his owner's racing colors.

Seabiscuit (Foaled 1933)

SEABISCUIT WAS A son of Hard Tack, himself a son of Man o' War. He was awkwardly built and didn't show much promise as a youngster. As a 2-year-old, he struggled. He raced 17 times before winning a race. During this losing streak, he could have been claimed for $2,500 more than once. All in all, he raced 35 times at 2, which is more than many horses race in their entire lives. As a 3-year-old, he ran in 10 unimportant races, winning two, before taking a claiming race at Saratoga. He wasn't claimed for the $6,000 tag that day, but the performance had caught the eye of a potential buyer, and he was purchased privately for $7,500 shortly thereafter.

By the time Seabiscuit turned 4, his career had begun to take off. He started the year by capturing the Huntington Beach Handicap at Santa Anita, a prep race for the $100,000 Santa Anita Handicap. Seabiscuit lost the big race by a nose, but he won 10 of his next 11 starts, all stakes races, and was named champion older horse. At age 5, he won 6 of 11 races and was voted Horse of the Year, largely on the strength of his victory over favored War Admiral in a memorable match race at Pimlico.

War Admiral (Foaled 1934)

WAR ADMIRAL, ANOTHER son of Man o' War, may have been one of the greatest horses of the century. As a 3-year-old, he ran in eight races and won all of them. He swept the Triple Crown and became Horse of the Year, beating out Seabiscuit in the voting. At 4, he won 9 of his 11 starts. There was tremendous public interest in a showdown between War Admiral and the 5-year-old Seabiscuit, and the two finally met in the 1938 Pimlico Special, which was run as a match race. It took place at Pimlico Race Course in Baltimore in front of a record crowd of 40,000. Seabiscuit got away faster from the walk-up start, which was unexpected. War Admiral quickly caught up, however, and at one point looked as if he were going to win. Then, with a sudden acceleration, Seabiscuit pulled powerfully away from his archrival at the top of the stretch for the victory. This impressive win assured Seabiscuit Horse of the Year honors.

Citation (Foaled 1945)

CITATION IS CONSIDERED by many to be the greatest Thoroughbred of all time. He became racing's first millionaire, went 16 straight races without defeat, and won the Triple Crown. He was owned by Warren Wright's powerful Calumet Farm and trained by "the Jones Boys"—Ben Jones and his son, Jimmy. "Plain Ben" Jones was credited with winning a record six Kentucky Derbies. Citation had a successful 2-year-old season, but really shone as a 3-year-old. He won stakes race after stakes race, including a sweep of the 1948 Triple Crown. By the end of his 3-year-old season, he had 27 wins in 29 starts, with two second-place finishes. In December 1948 he suffered an ankle injury that caused him to miss more than a year, and when he came back he was not as dominant, but Citation finally won his last three races and was retired with $1,085,760 in career earnings.

Kelso (Foaled 1957)

KELSO ACHIEVED THE seemingly impossible: He was elected Horse of the Year five times in a row (1960 through 1964). By the time he finished his career, he had set many track and course records. He compiled 39 wins, 12 second-place finishes, and two third-place finishes in 63 starts. Kelso, who was gelded as a young horse, only raced three times at 2. As a 3-year old, he didn't even run his first race of the year until two weeks after the Triple Crown was over. Despite his late start, he was still elected Horse of the Year.

In his 4-year old campaign, Kelso won a number of prestigious races, including the Suburban and Brooklyn Handicaps and The

Jockey Club Gold Cup. He was again voted Horse of the Year. As a 5-year-old he lost three of his first four starts and missed some time because of a virus. He regained his form in the fall, however, and won three stakes in a row, including The Jockey Club Gold Cup for the third straight year, thereby securing another Horse of the Year title.

Kelso was again voted Horse of the Year at 6. As a 7-year-old, he continued his winning ways while taking his fifth Jockey Club Gold Cup in a row. The Horse of the Year honor was once again his. Kelso won three of his six starts the next year, then he raced once in 1966, at the age of 9, before being retired. He lived out his days as a hunter and pleasure horse on his owner's farm in Maryland.

Forego (Foaled 1970)

FOREGO DID NOT start racing until his 3-year-old season and did not win a stakes race until late November. As a 4-year old, he really started to flourish. He won his first four starts, all stakes races, and finished out the year by winning the Woodward, the Vosburgh, and The Jockey Club Gold Cup, earning Eclipse Awards as champion older horse, sprinter, and Horse of the Year. He repeated as Horse of the Year in 1975 and 1976. Forego won 34 of 57 lifetime starts despite some chronic leg problems. The gutsy gelding was finally forced into retirement in the summer of 1978.

Secretariat (Foaled 1970)

SECRETARIAT WAS PERHAPS the best-known of all great Thoroughbreds. Even people who are not racing fans have heard of him. He was the only nonhuman ever to grace the cover of *Sports Illustrated* and is considered one of the most respected and well-liked equines in the history of the sport. He possessed superior ability and had an engaging personality to match.

From the beginning, Secretariat looked and acted like a winner. His first race was not a success (he was bumped early on), but he was sent out 11 days later and won a maiden race by six lengths. From that point on his career exploded, and he went on to win Horse of the Year honors as a 2-year-old. His 3-year-old season was remarkable, and one of the highlights was his stunning performance in the 1973 Kentucky Derby. Secretariat won easily by 2 ½ lengths and set a track record of 1:59 ⅖. Two weeks later in the Preakness, the second leg of the Triple Crown, Secretariat made a powerful move on the first turn and the rest was history. When he took the track for the Belmont Stakes, the third and final leg, he was attempting to become the first Triple Crown winner since Citation in 1948. Although he was favored to win, no one could have predicted how amazing his Belmont victory would be. Secretariat won by an astounding margin of 31 lengths in a world-record time of 2:24. He had already locked up his second Horse of the Year title, but he added to his accomplishments by beating older horses in the Marlboro Cup and winning two major stakes races on the grass. He was retired to stud at Claiborne Farm, where he became a successful sire and a constant favorite with visitors to the farm.

Fun Fact

Just prior to winning the Triple Crown, Secretariat appeared on the covers of three national magazines in the same week: *Newsweek, Sports Illustrated,* and *Time.*

Seattle Slew (Foaled 1974)

SEATTLE SLEW DID not have the most sought-after pedigree and was something of an ugly duckling as a youngster, so he brought only $17,500 at auction as a yearling. As a 2-year-old, however, he easily won all three of his starts, including the Champagne Stakes, and was named champion 2-year-old. Although he was still undefeated going into the Kentucky Derby, "Slew" had many doubters. Some felt that he was a one-dimensional front-runner who had never shown any true courage or versatility. Nevertheless, he cruised to victories in the Derby, Preakness, and Belmont Stakes, becoming the first undefeated winner of the Triple Crown.

After suffering his first loss, a fourth-place finish in the Swaps Stakes at Hollywood Park, Seattle Slew was given a well-deserved rest for the remainder of the season. The year following his Triple Crown success was a difficult one for the talented colt. Because of illness and injury, he was sidelined for 10 months. In addition, his original trainer, William Turner Jr., had been replaced by Douglas Peterson. By the fall of 1978, however, Seattle Slew regained his top form. In the first-ever meeting of Triple Crown winners, he defeated the 3-year-old Affirmed in the Marlboro Cup at Belmont Park, reestablishing his greatness.

Affirmed and Alydar (Foaled 1975)

IT IS DIFFICULT to mention Affirmed without mentioning his famous rival, Alydar. These two horses were the stars of an ongoing drama and held the attention of racing fans throughout the exciting 1978 season.

Affirmed was an elegant-looking colt, but not as well-bred as Alydar. Of the seven races that Affirmed won by a half-length or less during his career, Alydar finished second in five. In 1978, Affirmed had won the Kentucky Derby by a length and a half over Alydar and then edged him by only a neck in the Preakness. With a win in the Belmont Stakes, he would secure the Triple Crown. Alydar's trainer decided to switch tactics against Affirmed, and he removed Alydar's blinkers in the hope that this would encourage his colt to stay closer to the pace. Affirmed's opening half-mile in the Belmont was slow, and Alydar was sent up to challenge him earlier than usual. The two colts raced together to the wire, with Affirmed narrowly defeating Alydar to become the 11th (and through 2001, the last) Triple Crown winner in history. Alydar, who might have been a Triple Crown winner himself in many other years, also has a place in history as one of the most famous runners-up in sports.

John Henry (Foaled 1975)

JOHN HENRY DID not have a prestigious pedigree or particularly impressive conformation. He was sold as a yearling for $1,100, then sold again as a 2-year old for $2,200. His owner decided to geld him because he had a temper, which made him difficult to control. As a 3-year-old, he was still running in claiming races when he made his first start on the grass. He won by 14 lengths, a sign of things to come. Although John Henry won many important races on both dirt and turf in his career, he is probably best remembered as a turf horse, since he was a four-time champion in that category. At the age of 6, he won the inaugural Arlington Million and was subsequently named Horse of the Year. Over the next two years he raced less because of injuries, but was still named champion turf male in 1983. In 1984, at the age of 9, he won his second Arlington Million, and his second Horse of the Year title.

Fun Fact

Everyone has a favorite race or favorite horse. *Daily Racing Form* national correspondent Jay Privman had an affinity for a horse named Flawlessly. She was a champion female turf runner twice in the early 1990's. Privman liked her because she had a big white blaze down her face and was very distinctive looking.

Spectacular Bid (Foaled 1976)

SPECTACULAR BID, A very talented colt by Bold Bidder, compiled an impressive record of 26 wins from 30 starts. His trainer, Bud Delp, once called him "the best horse ever to look through a bridle." He was a champion at 2 and then waltzed through his first seven starts at 3 virtually unchallenged, winning the Kentucky Derby and the Preakness. Spectacular Bid finished third in the Belmont Stakes and failed to sweep the Triple Crown, but he rebounded to win his next two starts impressively. The time had come for him to take on the older Affirmed, who had won the Triple Crown the previous year. The two met in the 1979 Jockey Club Gold Cup at Belmont Park. Spectacular Bid battled tooth-and-nail with Affirmed in what would become known as a classic stretch duel. In the end, however, Spectacular Bid's older foe would not be denied and edged away with a three-quarter-length victory. Spectacular Bid won his next 10 races, and was so dominant that the last of these, the Woodward, was a walkover—an event in which a horse literally has no competition and "walks over" the track.

Personal Ensign (Foaled 1984)

PERSONAL ENSIGN'S PEDIGREE included War Admiral on both the sire's and the dam's side. As a 2-year-old, she won her first two starts but then fractured a rear leg. Screws were inserted in the bone to hold it together, and after nearly a year off, she returned to win four consecutive races. In her third year of racing, she won her first six starts, beating males in the Whitney at Saratoga and defeating the talented filly Winning Colors, that year's Kentucky Derby winner, in the Maskette at Belmont Park. These two met again in the Breeders' Cup Distaff at Churchill Downs. In what may people consider one of the most thrilling moments in racing history, Personal Ensign edged out Winning Colors to win her 13th and final career start. With this victory, she became the first major horse in 80 years to retire undefeated. Personal Ensign just missed Horse of the Year honors, but was voted the Eclipse Award for champion older filly or mare.

Sunday Silence and Easy Goer (Foaled 1986)

THESE TWO GIFTED colts created one of the greatest rivalries in racing. Today, fans still debate the question of which one was the better horse. Regardless of where one stands, it is clear that the rivalry generated enormous excitement. The pair met four times during their careers and Sunday Silence won three out of those four meetings. Each time they ran against each other, the favorite lost. Easy Goer had a more successful 2-year-old season, winning four races in a row, which included two Grade I stakes. He was named champion 2-year-old colt. Sunday Silence got a late start as a 2-year-old, but did manage to win a race in his second attempt and quickly developed into a serious racehorse only a few months later.

The heated battles between these two colts took place during the Triple Crown series and the Breeders' Cup Classic. In the Kentucky Derby, Sunday Silence drew first blood with an easy win. Sunday Silence also went on to win the Preakness, but the race was a taxing effort for both colts. This time Easy Goer moved first and took the lead, but Sunday Silence caught up and raced head-and-head to the wire, eventually winning by a nose. Sunday Silence came into the Belmont on the verge of taking the Triple Crown, but this was Easy Goer's day. He swept by Sunday Silence and left him in the dust, drawing off to an eight-length victory. Their last meeting took place at Gulfstream Park in the Breeders' Cup Classic, where, in another stunningly close race, Sunday Silence pulled of a neck victory.

Many fans were hoping to see this rivalry continue through the two colts' 4-year-old seasons, but after a few more races both were retired due to injuries.

Cigar (Foaled 1990)

WHILE RACING PRIMARILY on the turf during his 3- and 4-year-old seasons, Cigar never showed any signs of developing into the tremendous racehorse he would later become. Despite his strong turf pedigree, it wasn't until Cigar switched permanently to the dirt that he really started to excel on the racetrack. Bill Mott, who took over Cigar's training when the colt was 4, did not immediately enter him in a dirt race, but when he did, Cigar won by eight lengths. That was the beginning of a winning streak that would span three seasons. As a 5-year-old, Cigar won the Breeders' Cup Classic, which was worth $3 million at the time. The following year, Cigar proved himself again, this time on foreign soil. He traveled 7,000 miles to win the Dubai World Cup, the richest race in the world.

More importantly, in August of that same year, Cigar had the opportunity to beat the great Citation's 16-race winning streak in the 1996 Pacific Classic at Del Mar. In front of a record crowd of 44,000, Cigar came up short. He finished second to Dare and Go, trained by Richard Mandella. Although he didn't beat Citation's record, Cigar still marked himself as one of the great horses of the century. He was a two-time Horse of the Year and retired with nearly $10 million in career earnings.

Appendix 1:

action: 1) A horse's manner of moving. 2) A term meaning wagering: *The horse took a lot of action.*

age: All Thoroughbreds celebrate their birthdays on January 1.

allowance race: A race for which the racing secretary drafts certain conditions to determine weights to be carried, based on the horse's age, sex, and previous races and/or money won.

also-eligible: A horse officially entered for a race, but not permitted to start unless the field is reduced by scratches below a specified number.

apprentice: Rider who has not ridden a certain number of winners within a specified period of time. Also known as a *bug,* from the asterisk used to denote the weight allowance such riders receive.

apprentice allowance: Weight concession given to an apprentice rider: usually 10 pounds until the fifth winner, seven pounds until the 35th winner, and five pounds for one calendar year from the 35th winner. Apprentices do not receive an allowance when riding in a stakes race.

backside: Stable area, dormitories, and often a track kitchen, chapel, and recreation area for stable employees. Also known as the *backstretch,* since it is usually located behind or near that portion of the racetrack.

backstretch: 1) Straight portion of the far side of the racing surface between the turns. 2) See *backside*.

bandages: Leg wraps used for support or protection against injury during a race or workout.

bar shoe: A horseshoe closed at the back to help support the heel of the foot. Often worn by horses with quarter cracks or bruised feet.

bay: A horse color that consists of a brown coat (which can range from a yellow-tan to a bright auburn) and a black mane and tail. The muzzle and lower legs are always black, except where white markings are present.

bit: A stainless-steel, rubber, or aluminum bar, attached to the bridle, that fits in the horse's mouth and is one of the means by which a jockey exerts guidance and control.

black: A horse color that is black, including the muzzle, flanks, mane, tail, and legs unless white markings are present.

bleeder: A horse that bleeds from the lungs when small capillaries that surround the lungs' air sacs (alveoli) rupture. The medical term is "exercise-induced pulmonary hemorrhage" (EIPH). The most common treatment is the use of the diuretic furosemide (Lasix).

blinkers: Cup-shaped devices that attach to a cloth hood and limit a horse's vision, sometimes used to prevent him from swerving from objects or other horses on either side.

blowout: A short, timed workout, usually one to three days before a race, designed to sharpen a horse's speed. Usually three-eighths or one-half mile in distance.

bolt: Sudden veering from a straight course, usually to the outside rail.

breaking his or her maiden: Horse or rider winning the first race of his or her career.

Breeders' Cup: Thoroughbred racing's year-end championship, inaugurated in 1984. Known as Breeders' Cup Day, it consists of eight races, effective with the 1999 season, when the Filly and Mare Turf was run for the first time. Through 1998, it consisted of seven races. The event is conducted on one day at a different racetrack each year with purses and awards totaling $13 million. The races are the:

$1 million Breeders' Cup Sprint, for 3-year-olds and up at six furlongs.

$1 million Breeders' Cup Juvenile Fillies, for 2-year-old fillies at $1\frac{1}{16}$ miles.

$2 million Breeders' Cup Distaff, for fillies and mares, 3-year-olds and up, at $1\frac{1}{8}$ miles.

$1 million Breeders' Cup Mile, for 3-year-olds and up at one mile on the turf.

$1 million Bessener Trust Breeders' Cup Juvenile, for 2-year-olds at $1\frac{1}{16}$ miles.

$1 million Breeders' Cup Filly and Mare Turf, for fillies and mares, 3-year-olds and up, at $1\frac{3}{8}$ miles on the turf.

$2 million Breeders' Cup Turf, for 3-year-olds and up, at $1\frac{1}{2}$ miles on the turf.

$4 million Breeders' Cup Classic, for 3-year-olds and up, at $1\frac{1}{4}$ miles.

breeze (breezing): Working a horse at a good pace, but without encouragement from the rider.

bridle: A piece of equipment, usually made of leather or nylon, that fits on a horse's head and is where other equipment, such as the bit and the reins, are attached.

broodmare: A filly or mare that has been bred and is used to produce foals.

bug boy: An apprentice rider.

bullet (work): The best workout time for a particular distance on a given day at a track. From the printer's "bullet" that precedes the time of the workout in listings. Also known as a *black-letter* work in some parts of the country.

Bute: Short for *phenylbutazone,* a nonsteroidal anti-inflammatory medication that is legal in most racing jurisdictions. Often known by the trade names Butazolidin and Butazone.

calk: A projection on the bottom of a horseshoe, similar to a cleat, intended to prevent slipping, especially on a wet track. Also known as a *sticker*. Sometimes incorrectly spelled *caulk*.

chalk: Wagering favorite in a race. The term dates from the days when on-track bookmakers would write current odds on a chalkboard.

check(ed): When a jockey slows a horse due to other horses impeding its progress.

chestnut: 1) A horse color that may vary from a red-yellow to golden-yellow. The mane, tail, and legs are usually variations of the coat color, except where white markings are present. 2) A horny growth on the inside of a horse's leg that is used in identification.

chute: Extension of backstretch or homestretch to permit a straight running start in a race as opposed to starting on or near a turn.

claiming: Process by which a licensed person may purchase a horse entered in a designated race for a predetermined price. When a horse has been claimed, its new owner assumes title after the starting gate opens although the former owner is entitled to all purse money earned in that race.

claiming race: A race in which each horse entered is eligible to be purchased at a set price. Claims must be made before the race and only by licensed owners or their agents who have a horse registered to race at that meeting or who have received a claim certificate from the stewards.

clubhouse turn: Generally, the turn on a racing oval that is closest to the clubhouse facility; usually the first turn after the finish line.

colt: An ungelded (entire) male horse 4 years old or younger.

condition book(s): A series of booklets issued by a racing secretary, which set forth conditions of races to be run at a particular racetrack.

conditions: The requirements of a particular race. These may include age, sex, money or races won, weight carried, and the distance of the race.

coupled (entry): Two or more horses running as an entry in a single betting unit.

cuppy (track): A dry and loose racing surface that breaks away under a horse's hooves.

dam: The female parent of a foal.

damsire (broodmare sire): The sire of a broodmare. Used in reference to the maternal grandsire of a foal.

dark bay or brown: A horse color that ranges from brown with areas of tan on the shoulders, head, and flanks, to a dark brown, with tan areas seen only on the flanks and/or muzzle. The mane, tail, and lower portions of the legs are always black unless white markings are present.

dogs: Rubber traffic cones (or a wooden barrier) placed at certain distances out from the inner rail of the track or turf course, when the surface is wet, muddy, soft, yielding, or heavy, to prevent horses from churning the footing along the rail during the workout period.

driving: A horse that is all out to win and under strong urging from the jockey.

dwelt: Means that a horse was extremely late in breaking from the gate.

Eclipse Awards: Thoroughbred racing's year-end awards, honoring the top horses and humans in several categories. The Eclipse Awards are presented by the National Thoroughbred Racing Association, *Daily Racing Form,* and the National Turf Writers Association. Eclipse Award winners are referred to as *champions.*

entry: Two or more horses with common ownership (or in some cases trained by the same trainer) that are paired as a single betting unit in one race and/or are placed together by the racing secretary as part of a *mutuel field.* Rules on entries vary from state to state. Also known as a *coupled entry.*

fast (track): Footing that is dry, even, and resilient.

field horse: One of the two or more starters running as a single betting unit (entry) in the *mutuel field.* The track linemaker usually designates a "field" when there are more starters in a race than there are positions on the tote board.

filly: Female horse 4 years old or younger.

firm (course): A condition of a turf course corresponding to *fast* on a dirt track. A firm, resilient surface.

flatten out: To slow considerably; describes a very tired horse.

frog: The V-shaped, shock-absorbing pad on the bottom of a horse's foot.

furlong: One-eighth of a mile, 220 yards, 660 feet.

furosemide: A medication used in the treatment of bleeders, commonly known under the trade name Lasix. It acts as a diuretic, reducing pressure on the capillaries.

gelding: A male horse of any age that has been neutered by having both testicles removed (gelded).

girth: An elastic-and-leather band, sometimes covered with sheepskin, that passes under a horse's belly and is connected to both sides of the saddle.

good (track): A dirt track that is almost *fast* or a turf course slightly softer than *firm*.

graded race: A designation established in 1973 to classify select stakes races, at the request of European racing authorities, who had set up group races two years earlier. Capitalized when used in race title (the Grade I Kentucky Derby). See *group race.*

gray: A horse color where the majority of the coat is a mixture of black and white hairs. The mane, tail, and legs may be either black or gray unless white markings are present. Starting with foals of 1993, the color classifications *gray* and *roan* were combined as *roan or gray.* See *roan.*

group race: Established in 1971 by racing organizations in Britain, France, Germany, and Italy to classify select stakes races outside North America. Collectively called *pattern races.* Equivalent to American graded races. Capitalized when used in race title (the Group 1 Epsom Derby). See *graded race.*

half-brother, half-sister: Horses out of the same dam but by different sires. Horses with the same sire and different dams are *not* considered half-siblings in Thoroughbred racing.

halter: Like a bridle, but lacking a bit. Used in handling horses around the stable and when they are not being ridden.

hand: Four inches. A horse's height is measured in hands and inches from the top of the shoulder (withers) to the ground. For example, 15.2 hands is 15 hands, 2 inches. Thoroughbreds typically range from 15 to 17 hands.

handicap: 1) A race for which the track handicapper assigns the weights to be carried. 2) To make selections on the basis of past performances.

handily: 1) Describes a horse running at close to top speed in a workout, under encouragement from the rider. 2) A comparatively easy winning effort in a race.

handle: Amount of money wagered in the parimutuels on a race, a program, during a meeting, or for a year.

heavy (track): Wettest possible condition of a turf course; not usually found in North America.

hock: A large joint just above the cannon bone in the rear leg. Corresponds to the level of the knee of the front leg.

horse: When reference is made to sex, a *horse* is an ungelded male 5 years old or older.

hotwalker: Person who walks horses to cool them out after workouts or races.

in the money: In betting terms, a horse that finishes first, second, or third.

inquiry: A review of a race to check into a possible infraction of the rules. Also, a sign flashed by officials on the tote board on such occasions. If lodged by a jockey, it is called an *objection*.

ITW: Intertrack wagering.

The Jockey Club: An organization dedicated to the improvement of Thoroughbred breeding and racing. Incorporated February 10, 1894, in New York City, The Jockey Club serves as North America's Thoroughbred registry, responsible for the maintenance of The American Stud Book, a register of all Thoroughbreds foaled in the United States, Puerto Rico, and Canada; and of all Thoroughbreds imported into those countries from jurisdictions that have a registry recognized by The Jockey Club and the International Stud Book Committee.

juvenile: a 2-year-old horse.

Lasix: See *furosemide.*

length: A measurement approximating the length of a horse, used to denote distance between horses in a race.

listed race: A stakes race just below a group race or graded race in quality.

maiden: 1) A horse or rider that has not won a race. 2) A female horse that has never been bred.

mare: Female horse 5 years old or older.

middle distance: Broadly, from one mile to 1 1/8 miles.

minus pool: A situation that results when a horse is so heavily played that, after deductions of state tax and commission, there is not enough money left to pay the legally prescribed minimum on each winning bet. The racing association usually makes up the difference.

morning line: Probable odds on each horse in a race, as determined by a mathematical formula used by the track handicapper, who tries to gauge both the ability of the horse and the likely final odds as determined by the bettors.

muddy (track): A condition of a racetrack that is wet but has no standing water.

mutuel field: See *field*.

name (of a Thoroughbred): Names of North American Thoroughbreds are registered by The Jockey Club. They can be no longer than 18 characters, including punctuation and spaces. The words *the, and, by, for, in* and *a* are almost always lowercase (for example, Love You by Heart; Go for Wand) unless one of them is the first word in the name (e.g., The Deputy).

noseband: A leather strap that fits over a horse's nose and helps secure the bridle. A "figure-eight" noseband goes over the nose and under the rings of the bit to help keep the horse's mouth closed. This keeps the tongue from sliding up over the bit and is used on horses that do not like having a *tongue tie* used.

objection: Claim of foul lodged by a rider, patrol judge, or other official after the running of a race. If lodged by an official, it is called an *inquiry*.

odds-on: Odds of less than even money.

off-track betting: Wagering conducted at or through legalized betting outlets usually run by the tracks, management companies specializing in parimutuel wagering, or, in New York State, by independent corporations chartered by the state. Wagers at these sites are usually commingled with on-track betting pools.

overlay: A horse going off at higher odds than it appears to warrant based on its past performances.

overweight: A horse carrying more weight than the conditions of the race require, usually because the jockey exceeds the stated limit.

paddock: Area where horses are saddled and paraded before being taken onto the track.

parimutuel(s): A form of wagering originated in 1865 by Frenchman Pierre Oller in which all money bet is divided up among those who have winning tickets, after taxes, takeout, and other deductions are made.

past performances: A horse's racing record, as presented through individual running lines, each of which details his performance in a specific race. Past performances were pioneered by *Daily Racing Form,* which publishes the most comprehensive version of these.

patrol judges: Officials who observe the progress of a race from various vantage points around the track.

phenylbutazone: See *Bute*.

photo finish: A result so close that it is necessary to use the finish-line camera to determine the order of finish.

pill: Small numbered ball used in a blind draw to decide post positions.

pinhooker: A person who buys a racehorse with the specific intention of reselling it at a profit.

place: Second position at the finish.

poles: Markers at measured distances around the track designating the distance from the finish. The quarter pole, for instance, is a quarter of a mile from the finish, not from the start.

post parade: The procession of horses as they pass the stands on their way from the paddock to the starting gate.

post position: The number of the stall in the starting gate from which a horse breaks.

post time: Designated time for a race to start.

purse: The total monetary amount distributed after a race to the owners of the entrants who have finished in the (usually) top four or five positions. Some racing jurisdictions may pay purse money through other places.

quarter crack: A crack in the hoof wall between the toe and the heel.

ridden out: A horse that finishes a race under mild urging; not as severe as *driving*.

roan: A horse color in which the majority of the coat is a mixture of red and white hairs or brown and white hairs. The mane, tail, and legs may be black, chestnut, or roan unless white markings are present. Starting with foals of 1993, the color classifications *gray* and *roan* were combined as *roan or gray*. See *gray*.

route: Broadly, a race distance of one mile or longer.

saddle: A Thoroughbred-racing saddle is the lightest saddle used, weighing less than two pounds.

scale of weights: Fixed weights to be carried by horses according to their age, sex, the race distance, and the time of year.

scratch: To be taken out of a race before it starts. Trainers usually scratch horses due to adverse track conditions or because of a change in a horse's health or soundness. The track's veterinarian can scratch a horse at any time.

shadow roll: A thick band, usually sheepskin, that is placed over the noseband of the bridle to keep the horse from seeing shadows on the track and shying away from or jumping them.

shed row: 1) The dirt corridor outside the stalls in a stable. Horses are often walked in the shed row before going to the track for exercise or afterward, while cooling out. 2) The line of stalls assigned to a particular trainer.

show: Third position at the finish.

silks: Jacket and cap worn by riders, in the racing colors of the horse's owner.

simulcast: A simultaneous live-television transmission of a race to other tracks, off-track betting offices, or other outlets for the purpose of wagering.

sire: 1) The male parent. 2) To beget foals.

sloppy (track): A racing strip that is saturated with water, with standing water visible.

slow (track): A racing strip that is wet on both the surface and base.

soft (track): Condition of a turf course with a large amount of moisture. Horses sink very deeply into it.

spit the bit: A term referring to a tired horse that begins to run less aggressively, backing off on the "pull" a rider normally feels on the reins from an eager horse. Also used as a generic term for an exhausted horse.

sprint: Short race, less than one mile.

stakes: A race for which the owner usually must pay a fee to run a horse. The fees, to which the track adds more money to make up the total purse, can be for nominating, maintaining eligibility, entering, and starting. Stakes races by invitation require no fees.

steadied: A horse being taken in hand by its rider, usually because of being in close quarters.

stewards: Officials of the race meeting responsible for enforcing the rules of racing.

stirrups: Metal D-shaped rings into which a jockey places his or her feet. They can be raised or lowered depending on the jockey's preference. Also known as *irons.*

stretch turn: Bend of track into the final straightaway.

Stud Book: Registry and genealogical record of Thoroughbreds, maintained by the Jockey Club of the country in question. For example, The American Stud Book.

taken up: A horse pulled up sharply by its rider because of being in close quarters.

tattoo: A permanent, indelible mark on the inside of the upper lip used to identify the horse.

Thoroughbred: A Thoroughbred traces back to one of the three "foundation sires"—the Darley Arabian, the Byerly Turk, or the Godolphin Barb—and has satisfied the rules and requirements of The Jockey Club and is registered in The American Stud Book or in a foreign stud book recognized by The Jockey Club and the International Stud Book Committee.

tongue tie (or strap): Strip of cloth-type material that is looped around a horse's tongue and tied to the lower jaw to prevent the horse from choking on his tongue in a race or workout, or to keep the tongue from sliding up over the bit, rendering the horse uncontrollable.

tote board: The (usually) electronic display board in the infield that reflects up-to-the-minute odds. It may also show the amounts wagered in each mutuel pool as well as information such as post time, minutes to post, fractional times, final time, order of finish, payoffs, jockey and equipment changes, etc.

track bias: A racing surface that favors a particular running style or position, e.g., front-runners or horses running on the inside.

Triple Crown: Used generically to denote a series of three important races, but is always capitalized when referring to historical races for 3-year-olds: in the United States, the Kentucky Derby, Preakness Stakes, and Belmont Stakes; in England, the 2000 Guineas, Epsom Derby, and St. Leger Stakes; in Canada, the Queen's Plate, Prince of Wales Stakes, and Breeders' Stakes.

washed out: A horse that becomes so nervous that it sweats profusely. Also known as *washy* or *lathered (up)*.

weanling: A foal that is less than a year old that has been separated (weaned) from its dam.

white: A horse color, extremely rare, in which all the hairs are white. The horse's eyes are brown, not pink, as would be the case with an albino.

withers: Area above the shoulder, where the neck meets the back.

World Thoroughbred Championship: A supporting brand for a Breeders' Cup that describes what the event has come to: A day of international races that largely determine Thoroughbred Racings year-end Champions.

yearling: A horse in its second calendar year of life, beginning January 1 of the year following its birth.

yielding: Condition of a turf course with a great deal of moisture. Horses sink into it noticeably.

Appendix 2:

AQUEDUCT
Address: P.O. Box 90, Jamaica, New York 11417
Telephone: (718) 641-4700
Web Site: *www.nyra.com/aqueduct*

ARLINGTON PARK
Address: P.O. Box 7, Arlington Heights,
   Illinois 60006
Telephone: (847) 385-7500
Web Site: *www.arlingtonpark.com*

ATLANTIC CITY RACE COURSE
Address: 4501 Black Horse Pike, Mays Landing,
   New Jersey 08330
Telephone: (609) 641-2190
Web Site: None

BAY MEADOWS
Address: P.O. Box 5050, San Mateo,
   California 94402
Telephone: (650) 574-RACE
Web Site: *webmaster@baymeadows.com*

BELMONT PARK
Address: P.O. Box 90, Jamaica, New York 11417
Telephone: (718) 641-4700
Web Site: *www.nyra.com/belmont*

BEULAH PARK
Address: 3664 Grant Avenue, Grove City,
   Ohio 43123
Telephone: (614) 871-9600
Web Site: *www.beulahpark.com*

CALDER RACE COURSE
Address: P.O. Box 1808, Miami, Florida
   33055-0808
Telephone: (305) 625-1311
Web Site: *www.calderracecourse.com*

CANTERBURY PARK
Address: 1100 Canterbury Road, Shakopee,
   Minnesota 55379
Telephone: (952) 445-7223
Web Site: *www.canterburypark.com*

CHURCHILL DOWNS
Address: 700 Central Avenue, Louisville,
   Kentucky 40208-1200
Telephone: (502) 636-4400
Web Site: *www.kentuckyderby.com*

COLONIAL DOWNS
Address: 10515 Colonial Downs Parkway, New
   Kent, Virginia 23124
Telephone: (804) 966-7223
Web Site: *www.colonialdowns.com*

DELAWARE PARK
Address: 777 Delaware Park Blvd., Wilmington,
    Delaware
Telephone: (302) 994-2521
Web Site: www.delpark.com

DEL MAR
Address: P.O. Box 700, Del Mar, California 92014
Telephone: (858) 755-1141
Web Site: www.delmarracing.com

ELLIS PARK
Address: P.O. Box 33, Henderson, Kentucky
    42419-0033
Telephone: (812) 425-1456
Web Site: www.ellisparkracing.com

FAIR GROUNDS
Address: P.O. Box 52529, New Orleans, Louisiana
    70152
Telephone: (504) 944-5515
Web Site: www.fgno.com

FINGER LAKES
Address: P.O. Box 25250, Farmington, New York
    14425
Telephone: (716) 924-3232
Web Site: www.fingerlakesracetrack.com

FONNER PARK
Address: P.O. Box 490, Grand Island, Nebraska
    68802-0490
Telephone: (308) 382-4515
Web Site: www.fonnerpark.com

GULFSTREAM PARK
Address: 901 South Federal Highway, Hallandale,
    Florida 33009
Telephone: (954) 454-7000
Web Site: www.gulfstreampark.com

HASTINGS PARK RACECOURSE
Address: Hastings Park Racecourse, Vancouver,
    B.C., Canada V5K 3N8
Telephone: (604) 254-1631
Web Site: www.hastingspark.com

HAWTHORNE RACE COURSE
Address: 3501 S. Laramie Avenue,
    Stickney/Cicero, Illinois 60804
Telephone: (708) 780-3700
Web Site: www.hawthorneracecourse.com

HORSEMEN'S PARK
Address: 6303 "Q" Street, Omaha, Nebraska
    68117
Telephone: (402) 731-2900
Web Site: www.horsemenspark.com

KEENELAND
Address: P.O. Box 1690, Lexington, Kentucky
    40588-1690
Telephone: (859) 254-3412
Web Site: www.keeneland.com

LAUREL PARK
Address: Racetrack Road and Route 198, Laurel,
    Maryland 20725
Telephone: (301) 725-0400
Web Site: www.marylandracing.com

LONE STAR PARK
Address: 1000 Lone Star Parkway, Grand Prairie,
    Texas 75050
Telephone: (972) 263-RACE
Web Site: www.lonestarpark.com

LOUISIANA DOWNS
Address: P.O. Box 5519, Bossier City, Louisiana
    71171-5519
Telephone: (318) 742-5555
Web Site: www.ladowns.com

THE MEADOWLANDS
Address: 50 Route 120, East Rutherford, New
    Jersey 07073
Telephone: (201) 935-8500
Web Site: www.thebigm.com

MONMOUTH PARK
Address: 175 Oceanport Avenue, Oceanport,
    New Jersey 07757
Telephone: (732) 222-5100
Web Site: www.monmouthpark.com

MOUNTAINEER PARK
Address: P.O. Box 358, Route 2 South Chester,
    WV 26034
Telephone: (304) 387-8300/8000
Web Site: www.mtrgaming.com

NORTHLANDS PARK
Address: Box 1480, Edmonton, AB, T5J 2N5
Telephone: (780) 471-7379
Web Site: www.northlands.com/npracing

OAKLAWN PARK
Address: P.O. Box 699, Hot Springs, Arkansas
   71902
Telephone: (501) 623-4411
Web Site: *www.oaklawn.com*

PENN NATIONAL RACE COURSE
Address: P.O. Box 32, Grantville, Pennsylvania
   17028
Telephone: (717) 469-2211
Web Site: *www.pennnational.com*

PHILADELPHIA PARK
Address: P.O. Box 1000, Bensalem, Pennsylvania
   19020-2096
Telephone: (215) 639-9000
Web Site: *www.philadelphiapark.com*

PIMLICO RACE COURSE
Address: Maryland Jockey Club, Pimlico Race
   Course, Baltimore, Maryland 21215
Telephone: (410) 466-2521
Web Site: *www.marylandracing.com*

PLAYFAIR
Address: East Main and North Altamont,
   Spokane, WA 99202
Telephone: (509) 534-0505
Web Site: *www.playfairracing.com*

PLEASANTON
Address: 4501 Pleasanton Avenue, Pleasanton,
   CA 94566
Telephone: (925) 426-7600
Web Site: *www.calfairs.com*

PORTLAND MEADOWS
Address: 1001 N. Schmeer Rd., Portland, Oregon
   97217
Telephone: (503) 285-9144
Web Site: *www.portlandmeadows.com*

PRAIRIE MEADOWS
Address: P.O. Box 1000, Altoona, Iowa 50009
Telephone: (515) 967-1000
Web Site: *www.prairiemeadows.com*

REMINGTON PARK
Address: One Remington Place, Oklahoma City,
   Oklahoma 73111
Telephone: (405) 424-1000
Web Site: *www.remingtonpark.com*

RETAMA PARK
Address: P.O. Box 47535, San Antonio, TX
   78265-7535
Telephone: (210) 651-7000
Web Site: *www.retamapark.com*

RILLITO PARK
Address: P.O. Box 65132, Tucson, Arizona 85718
Telephone: (520) 293-5011
Web Site: None

RIVER DOWNS
Address: P.O. Box 30286, Cincinnati, Ohio
   45230-0286
Telephone: (513) 232-8000
Web Site: *www.riverdowns.com*

ROCKINGHAM PARK
Address: P.O. Box 47, Salem,
   New Hampshire 03079
Telephone: (603) 898-2311
Web Site: *www.rockinghampark.com*

RUIDOSO DOWNS
Address: P.O. Box 449, Ruidoso Downs, New
   Mexico 88346
Telephone: (505) 378-4431
Web Site: *www.ruidownsracing.com*

SACRAMENTO
Address: 1600 Exposition Boulevard,
   Sacramento, CA 95815
Telephone: (916) 263-3000
Web Site: *www.calfairs.com*

SAM HOUSTON RACE PARK
Address: 7575 North Sam Houston Pkwy. West,
   Houston, Texas 77064
Telephone: (281) 807-8700
Web Site: *www.shrp.com*

SANTA ANITA PARK
Address: Los Angeles Turf Club, Santa Anita
   Park, P.O. Box 60014, Arcadia, California
   91066-6014
Telephone: (626) 574-7223
Web Site: *www.santaanita.com*

SANTA ROSA
Address: 1350 Bennett Valley Road, Santa Rosa,
   CA 95403
Telephone: (707) 545-4200
Web Site: www.calfairs.com

SARATOGA RACE COURSE
Address: New York Racing Association Inc., P.O.
   Box 90, Jamaica, New York 11417
Telephone: (718) 641-4700
Web Site: www.nyra.com

SOLANO
Address: 900 Fairgrounds Drive, Vallejo, CA
   94585
Telephone: (707) 644-4401
Web Site: www.calfairs.com

SPORTSMAN'S PARK
Address: 3301 Laramie Avenue, Cicero, Illinois
   60804
Telephone: (773) 242-1121
Web Site: www.sportsmanspark.com

STOCKTON
Address: 1658 South Airport Way, Stockton,
   CA 95205
Telephone: (209) 466-5041
Web Site: www.calfairs.com

SUFFOLK DOWNS
Address: 111 Waldemar Avenue, East Boston,
   Massachusetts 02128
Telephone: (617) 567-3900
Web Site: http://www.suffolkdowns.com/

SUNLAND PARK
Address: P.O. Box 1, Sunland Park, New Mexico
   88063
Telephone: (505) 874-5200
Web Site: www.sunland-park.com

SUN RAY PARK
Address: 39 Road 5568, Farmington, New Mexico
   87401 1466
Telephone: (505) 326-4898
Web Site: www.nmracing.com/sunray.htm

TAMPA BAY DOWNS
Address: P.O. Box 2007, Oldsmar, Florida 34677
Telephone: (813) 855-4401
Web Site: www.tampadowns.com

THISTLEDOWN
Address: P.O. Box 28280, Cleveland, Ohio 44128
Telephone: (216) 662-8600
Web Site: www.thistledown.com

TIMONIUM
Address: Maryland State Fair, P.O. Box 188,
   Timonium, Maryland 21094
Telephone: (410) 252-0200
Web Site: www.marylandstatefair.com

TURF PARADISE
Address: 1501 West Bell Road, Phoenix, Arizona
   85023
Telephone: (602) 942-1101
Web Site: www.turfparadise.com

TURFWAY PARK
Address: P.O. Box 8, Florence, Kentucky 41042
Telephone: (859) 371-0200
Web Site: www.turfwaypark.com

WILL ROGERS DOWNS
Address: 20900 So. 4200 Road, Claremore, OK
   74017
Telephone: (918) 343-5900
Web Site: www.willrogersdowns.com

WOODBINE
Address: P.O. Box 156, Rexdale, Ontario, Canada
   M9W 5L2
Telephone: (416) 675-6110
Web Site: www.ojc.com

WOODLANDS
Address: P.O. Box 12036, Kansas City, Kansas
   66112
Telephone: (913) 299-3636
Web Site: None

About the Author

AUTHOR AND SPORTS marketer Betsy Berns has dedicated her professional career to making sports more accessible and enjoyable. She is the author of *The Female Fan Guide to Pro Football* as well as *The Female Fan Guide to Motorsports*. Berns has served as a consultant to the National Football League and designed and implemented contests searching for sports' ultimate female fans.™ She has also written for, or been featured in, *USA Today, Sport* magazine, *Extra, ABC World News Tonight,* Fox News Channel, and Comedy Central. Berns has conducted over 300 radio and TV interviews and has been the subject of a Lifetime television special profiling women in sports.

Berns has an MBA from the J. L. Kellogg Graduate School of Management of Northwestern University and a bachelor's degree from Claremont McKenna College.